The Sacraments

Brent D. Peterson

THE FOUNDRY
PUBLISHING

Copyright © 2024 by Brent D. Peterson

The Foundry Publishing®
PO Box 419527
Kansas City, MO 64141
thefoundrypublishing.com

ISBN 978-0-8341-4251-0

Cover design: Arthur Cherry
Interior design: Sharon Page

Library of Congress Cataloging-in-Publication Data
A complete catalog record for this book is available from the Library of Congress.

The internet addresses, email addresses, and phone numbers in this book are accurate at the time of publication. They are provided as a resource. The Foundry Publishing® does not endorse them or vouch for their content or permanence.

Contents

Introduction

The sacraments are God's gift to the church that allow us to participate in the further redemption of creation. While this book can stand alone in its exploration of the sacraments of baptism and the Lord's Supper, it lives within the theological imagination of a *martyr ecclesiology* that was considered in a prior volume in this series on *The Church*. That book celebrated that *the church is the eschatological being and becoming of the body of Jesus Christ, who was crucified and buried, who is resurrected and ascended.* As such in the Wesleyan tradition, this conversation celebrates a martyr ecclesiology as the people participate in the new creation God is working in the world for the redemption of all things.

A Wesleyan soteriological lens frames this entire conversation on communal worship broadly, and then specifically, regarding the sacraments of baptism and the Lord's Supper. This sacramental conversation considers both a robust theology as well as faithful sacramental practice in the local church. Finally, within the great rhythm of God gathering (inhaling) the church for communal worship (Word and sacraments), God then sends (exhales) the church out from communal worship to live into our vocation as the body of Christ in the world as our doxological mission.

This conversation draws upon a generous orthodoxy across all of Christianity while also being saturated by a Wesleyan eschatological hope and optimism of grace. God created humans and all creation so that love, joy, and goodness would flourish and so that creation may glorify (re-image) God. Creation's glorification of God, reflecting back God's light and love, illuminates the Pauline celebration of hope and praise that indeed God "may be all in all" (1 Corinthians 15:28). This is the divine *telos* (goal or aim) of love for creation.

Within this hope and goal of love, the Wesleyan tradition takes very seriously the devastating consequences of sin. For Wesleyans, love and sin are best understood relationally. While the dis-ease of sin constrains, tarnishes, and attempts to choke off love, the Wesleyan optimism of hope is that God refuses to allow sin, death, pain, and suffering to have the final word. This hope is not naïve to the brutal consequences of sin; it is instead an invitation to refuse the despairing perspective of doom that says sin and death eternally reign. Wesleyans affirm that God desires to partner with creation as full healing and maturity in love continues to come.

The full hope and vision of God's love always invites more redemption, more love, and more flourishing. Therefore, God invites and empowers a journey of healing from sin to love and reconciliation that leaves nothing behind as worthless. Moreover, God invites creation never to settle for convenient, easy, or partial transformations in love (Romans 12:1–2). God invites us to press into the full gift of redemption—creation's entire sanctification. In this life we are invited to participate in this ongoing journey toward that upward call in Christ Jesus (see Philippians 3:13–14). As the primary work of the martyr church, communal worship is an eschatological divine-human encounter that participates in God's kingdom coming more fully.

Communal worship is part of God's ordained, Spirit-empowered respiratory system. God gathers and *breathes in* individual believers so we can be reformed and remade, re-united as the body of the crucified and resurrected

Christ. After the dynamic rhythms of the communal worship encounter, the church is sent out—*exhaled* by and with the Spirit to participate in God's continual healing of creation. This movement out and into the world is part of the church's doxological mission and a further living into the fruitful transformation that God is working within the crucified and resurrected body.

The sacraments of baptism and the Lord's Supper will be explored as a further intensification of the divine-human encounter in communal worship. The revival occurring around John and Charles Wesley has often been called a *sacramental revival*. Although the Wesleys largely affirmed the sacramental theology of their contemporary Church of England, what was novel in their theology was their zeal to celebrate the sacraments not as dead formulaic rites but as a dynamic *means of grace.*

Baptism

Baptism is God's invitation to new birth as part of one's full initiation in the martyr church as the body of the crucified and resurrected Christ. Baptism is both a drowning and a cleansing. In baptism, the Spirit puts to death the deeds of darkness and sin. The disease of sin is vanquished as one joins in Christ's death. Similarly, as persons are joined to Christ's death, they are also raised in the newness of life (see Romans 6:1–6). Within this celebration, there are also pastoral best practices to consider in order to equip, empower, and encourage local churches to live into the gift and healing of baptism more fully.

While baptism puts sin to death and raises persons to new life, there becomes a unique ecclesial and communal anthropology that marks Christians collectively as the church. For many Christians living in Europe and the United States, a strong sense of individualism permeates most aspects of culture, but it is dangerous to co-opt the

Christian gospel with individualistic libertarianism. The sacrament of baptism declares that individuals find fulfillment as part of the martyr church. Thinking individually versus communally also informs the eschatological hope one imagines and the ethics for how one lives into such a future. Practice shapes imagination, and imagination shapes practice. Christians living in individualism-centered cultures may need to work more intentionally to find their identity not in themselves, isolated and abstracted from others, but in the crucified and resurrected Christ.

Eucharist

John and Charles Wesley's zeal for eucharistic celebration was central to their own formation from their days at Oxford, and it was central for the Methodist revival and renewal within the Church of England. The issues of presence, sacrifice, and mission will form the outline of our theological conversation on the Lord's Supper.

Presence and sacrifice in the celebration of the Eucharist have unfortunately caused division among Christian traditions since the Reformation. Too often, debates have focused only on how Christ is present at the Table. While Christ's presence is crucial, considering the congregation's presence is also a critical part of the divine-human encounter. Another point of division has been the question of sacrifice. The Wesleyan tradition affirms a dynamic sense that each Lord's Supper is a sacrificial event and encounter.

Finally, the eucharistic conversation will consider what it means for the church to be sent out missionally as the body of the crucified and resurrected Christ. This movement by and with the Spirit is part of the church's ongoing doxological formation participating in God's further inbreaking of God's new creation kingdom. This holy work participates in the full sacramental fruitfulness and flourishing.

After the theological eucharistic discourse, some best practices for local churches will also be explored. Pastoral issues around frequency, fencing the table, who can preside and serve, the elements themselves, liturgies, and more will be considered.

Sacred Grace

This entire sacramental conversation celebrates the continual becoming of the church as the body of the crucified and resurrected Christ. These practices within the Wesleyan tradition celebrate divine-human encounters whereby the triune God seeks to heal and mature persons in love—a recovery and restoration of the image of God. This healing and maturation are not simply for individuals but are a further participation in the inbreaking of the kingdom of God.

Finally, it is important that this text be received as a gift without condemnation. The broader Wesleyan tradition has not always trained pastors and congregations well regarding the significance of the sacraments. Both the theological discourse and the best practices may illuminate previously held less-than-ideal ideas or practices. Such revelation should not yield guilt but offer new hope, insight, and encouragement for a more robust sacramental celebration in the ongoing formation of the martyr church of Jesus Christ.

Editorial Note: Terms that are defined in the glossary are bolded the first time they appear in the book following the introduction.

A Wesleyan Imagination

To begin this conversation, attention will be given to the unique Wesleyan lens that shapes this entire volume. The sacraments fall centrally within a Wesleyan celebration of salvation. Tracing the Wesleyan sacramental fervor through the journey of the Wesley brothers sets an important foundation.

While there is fertile theological soil to be tilled and faithful practice from church tradition to soak in, it is important to begin by *remembering* God's ongoing story and work in creation. Without care, sacraments and communal worship can become disembodied practices that are disconnected from God's continual work of creation, healing, and redemption in the world. Those who are antsy to get immediately to the specific discussions on the sacraments of the Lord's Supper and baptism are welcome to skip ahead. However, this section seeks to provide an important theological foundation and imagination that both grounds and liberates the wonderful gifts of the sacraments God has given to the martyr church.

Finally, this section will explore the unique aspects of salvation through a focus on the unity and particularity of prevenient, justifying, and sanctifying grace.

13

ONE

A Wesleyan Aroma in Creation

How should one begin a conversation on communal worship and specifically on the divine-human encounters of the **sacraments** and the subsequent missional holy work embodied for the life of the world?

All storytellers write from a unique viewpoint. This text is simply telling a story of God and of God's people at work in the world participating in the new creation kingdom that is coming more each day. As such, this text on the sacraments will be written with a Wesleyan lens, considering both John and Charles Wesley as well as their liturgical and theological heirs. The Wesley brothers saw themselves as part of the church **catholic** (or universal church) and thus celebrated and largely affirmed not only theology and practices of the Church of England but also that tradition's connection back to the early mothers and fathers of the church. In addition, the ongoing Wesleyan tradition has learned and should learn from all parts of the Christian faith in the continual celebration and illumination of these blessed mysteries of the sacraments.

Some may wonder if such a pedagogical rubric will result in a bland ecumenicism. Conversely, the Wesleyan tradition celebrates that God is at work revealing and healing *all* parts of creation. Thus, with an eye of discernment, a Wesleyan hospitality seeks in hope to encounter and be encountered by God's revelations and insights regarding the sacraments from the Christian church broadly. Within this general spirit of learning and listening, we admit that there are unique aspects specifically from the Wesleyan tradition, which we will highlight with the label *Wesleyan Sacramental Theology*. This emphasis will be one of distinction without disdain. Although there are differences in theology and practice among the various traditions, Wesleyans do not claim arrogant superiority over other traditions.

Created in Love, For Love

The Christian tradition bears witness not only to the power, joy, love, and blessing of God's creation but also to the God who continues to participate in the ongoing becoming of creation. Genesis 1 celebrates a daily divine affirmation of creation: "It is good." In the early narratives of Genesis and beyond is the affirmation that not only humans but also the rest of creation break forth in praise to God (see Isaiah 55:12). The goodness of creation, including humanity, is never in question.

The early texts of Genesis proclaim an idea that is woven throughout the whole Bible: humans are created to love God, love other humans, be loved by God and by others, love themselves, and take responsibility for creation by participating in creation's ongoing flourishing. The kind of love God offers to and expects from humanity is a love of covenantal joy, responsibility, and vocation. In *Confessions*, Augustine celebrates that humans are created to worship God. As a prayer, he yearns that humanity "cannot be content unless we praise you, because you made us for yourself and our hearts find no peace until they rest in you."[1] Moreover, The Westminster Shorter Catechism's first question asks, *What is the chief end of humanity?* It answers that humanity's

---

1. Saint Augustine, *Confessions*, Book 1.1 (New York: Penguin Books, 1961), 21.

"chief end is to glorify God, and to enjoy him forever."[2] This focus on God is the hope and *telos* (ultimate purpose) not only for humanity but also all of creation.

Within God's desire for love to flourish in all creation, the intrusion of sin and death work against the hope of life and love, bursting forth from the garden story in a pandemic[3] across the created order. Sin is not simply misbehaving, or breaking a law or divine command. Sin fractures relationships because it is a failure to love. Sin is not about the mere act of lying, cheating, or stealing; it is always grounded in relational wrenching: whom did I lie to, whom did I cheat, whom did I steal from? This pandemic of sin not only infected humanity in the garden but also the rest of creation: "We know that the whole creation is groaning together and suffering labor pains up until now. And it's not only the creation. We ourselves who have the Spirit as the first crop of the harvest also groan inside as we wait to be adopted and for our bodies to be set free" (Romans 8:22–23).

The Wesleyan tradition affirms that God does not desire to leave any in a place of death and sin but instead desires that all may find healing, life, and reconciling love (see 2 Peter 3:9). Scripture records the calling of Abram and Sarai to be a unique people who embody the way of God in order to bless all the families of the earth (see Genesis 12:3). God gave this unique people the law through Moses as a guide to image and reflect the way of Yahweh on the earth. Paul notes that, while the law could demonstrate the

---

2. The Presbytery of the United States, Free Church of Scotland (Continuing), "The Westminster Shorter Catechism," https://www.westminsterconfession.org /resources/confessional-standards/the-westminster-shorter-catechism/.

3. It is tempting to refer to sin as endemic, a medical term that indicates a disease that will never be fully eradicated. However, the term "pandemic" intentionally celebrates the Christian hope that, although sin is so far-reaching as to be global, it is not eternal, and one day it *will* cease to be.

right way of God, it did not have the power to help persons follow it completely on their own. Paul notes that the law did well to show the sin that infects all humans (see Romans 3:23; 7:7–12). Yet, as a fulfillment of God's promise in love not to leave humanity sick unto death, God the Father sent the Son to be incarnated in Jesus Christ by the power of the Spirit. As celebrated in the volume in this series on *The Church*, Jesus Christ inaugurates and embodies the irruption of the kingdom of God on earth and offers reconciliation with all creation to be healed and set free from sin into the divine dance (***perichoresis***) of triune love.

Christ is the foundation of the martyr church as the body of the crucified and resurrected Holy One. Beginning with Abram and Sarai and moving forward, God desires to covenant with people not only as part of our ongoing healing from sin to love but in order that we participate with God, as clay in a potter's hand, in the further inbreaking of the kingdom of God.

After Christ ascends, the Spirit is poured out on the believers at Pentecost, and the church is most fully born of water and Spirit (see Acts 2). As the church moves forward, its mission is clear: continue to be used by God to participate in the further inbreaking of the kingdom of God. The church is sent to reach out to all persons drowning in despair, clinging to corruption, and saturated in sin—both from what they have done and what has been done to them. The good news declares healing and forgiveness and life, liberation from slavery to sin and the disease of death (see Romans 6).

The Gift of Salvation Invites and Empowers Response

A central affirmation of the gospel is that the gift of healing, salvation, and reconciliation offered by God the Father, through the ministry of Jesus Christ, by the pow-

Wesleyan Sacramental Theology

God continually makes the first move in reaching out to encounter and offer life in love. Yet God's love is not coercive or manipulative. By wooing and inviting, God empowers us to respond to God's invitation while also empowering that response.

er of the Holy Spirit is never something we can earn or achieve on our own. Although the law shows the way of life, we cannot attain it on our own power; we all fall short (see Romans 3:23). Yet the good news of salvation and healing is that God offers them as a gift. The apostle Paul celebrates this gift of salvation as central to the Christian gospel: "You are saved by God's grace because of your faith. This salvation is God's gift. It's not something you possessed. It's not something you did that you can be proud of. Instead, we are God's accomplishment, created in Christ Jesus to do good things. God planned for these good things to be the way that we live our lives" (Ephesians 2:8–10).

Not only does this passage celebrate God's gift of salvation, but it also declares the joy and hope we are as God's *accomplishment*, where we can do what we were created to do—good things, holy work, things of life, joy, and creation, allowing love to flourish in and through us. Within this gift of salvation, the Wesleyan tradition is also very clear that God does not simply choose to save us apart from our desire to be redeemed. God's wooing, *prevenient* invitation seeks our participation in the continual work of new creation God is doing.

Wesleyans follow the example of Jesus's interactions with people in the Gospels. Some responded well to Jesus's invitation to faith and discipleship, such as his chosen disciples, and Mary and Martha (see Mark 1:16–20; 2:13–14; Luke 10:38–42). Some, like the rich man in Mark, walked away from Jesus's invitation (see Mark 10:17–31). When we respond positively to God's invitation, such a response is always empowered by God and not a work that makes us worthy of the gift. Yet God desires to covenant and partner together in the ongoing healing of creation—not as partners equal with God but as ambassadors of the kingdom of God (see 2 Corinthians 5:20).

Salvation as Healing

The gift of the sacraments is part of God's work in the world healing and redeeming persons as part of the new creation that is here and further coming. The Wesleyan tradition imagines salvation as the healing of humans and creation from the disease of sin. Randy Maddox's seminal work *Responsible Grace* asserts that salvation is first and foremost a therapeutic healing from sin to love—a recovery of Christlikeness in the **image of God**. This perspective grounds salvation as primarily relational rather than juridical (a legal decree).

Wesley certainly affirmed the power of God's justifying grace. **Justification** is God declaring persons righteous by faith through the life, death, and resurrection of Jesus. Justification is the legal change of position as declared by God through the forgiveness of sins. Yet Wesleyans believe that God desires to do more than simply *declare* us righteous through Christ. God seeks to *make* us righteous in the ongoing work of **sanctification**.

Maddox summarizes John Wesley's distinction by describing "justification as a *relative* change, in which God declares us forgiven by virtue of Christ, and sanctification as a *real* change in which the Spirit renews our fallen nature."[4] This distinction does not mean justification and sanctification are at odds; instead, they each provide unique prisms in celebrating the full promise and hope of Christian salvation.

A Holy Life as the Fruit of God's Love in Us

Although some Christians have been uncomfortable with the biblical book of James because of its emphasis on

---

4. Randy L. Maddox, *Responsible Grace: John Wesley's Practical Theology* (Nashville: Kingswood, 1994), 170.

Wesleyan Sacramental Theology

The difference between justification and sanctification is important. The sacraments not only participate in our juridical forgiveness (justification) but also serve as healing encounters of the triune God where we are invited to be more fully healed in love, moving into maturity in Christlikeness (sanctification).

the futility of faith without works, the Wesleyan tradition fully testifies to the importance of works of holy love as the fruit of God's healing in one's life. While the fruit of a holy life is never a work that earns our salvation, without the works of maturity in love, our faith is dead (see James 2:14–17). John Wesley grew pastorally annoyed and sad concerning Christian **nominalism** in England in the eighteenth century.[5] Many in England at that time considered their **baptism** to be merely a faith-related event in their past, but their lives did not bear the fruit of holy love. John and Charles Wesley's reformation and revival called believers into a holy and mature love that evidenced a dynamic faith continually at work in their lives.

Although the call to a holy life did lead some in the Wesleyan tradition to an unfortunate legalistic interpretation of works, the invitation to a holy life at its best allows the Spirit to do its full work both in each person and in the full redemption of all creation. A Wesleyan sacramental theology is central to this ongoing healing and maturing in love for the Wesleys.

Grace as God's Presence

We have discussed sin and salvation in the Wesleyan tradition as best understood relationally. In thinking about the salvation and healing God is working in creation, it is also important to consider how the *ordo salutis* (the way of salvation) grounds God's works in divine-human transformative encounters. One of the key distinctions of a Wesleyan sacramental theology is an acknowledgment of the sacraments as *means of grace.* In fact, John Wesley's sermon "Means of Grace" is one of the most helpful resources in discerning his understanding of the sacraments.

---

5. Nominal Christians are those who call themselves Christians but do not live in ways that set them apart as Christ followers.

"Grace" is a wonderful word used in Scripture and in songs of the faith, but what *is* **grace**? When I ask my students to help define grace, they rightly respond with ideas about *unconditional favor, gift,* and *undeserved healing.* All of these are wonderful, but they do not get to the heart of what the sacraments are as means of grace. To receive God's grace is not like God giving us a one-hundred-dollar bill. Grace is not an object of material substance. For the Wesleyan tradition, both in salvation and specifically when referring to the sacraments, grace should be understood as the undeserved, healing, and transforming *presence of the triune God.* Mildred Bangs Wynkoop emphasizes that, particularly in Wesleyan theology, grace must not be thought of as some object or thing that exists outside of God. "Grace is never impersonal or *something* apart from God himself."[6]

Affirming that God's transformational presence is an important part of a Wesleyan sacramental theology can anchor our sacramental conversation. In light of this exploration of the Wesleyan ethos and aroma, let's look at how the sacraments are central to a Wesleyan order of salvation.

---

6. Mildred Bangs Wynkoop, *A Theology of Love: The Dynamic of Wesleyanism* (Kansas City, MO: Beacon Hill Press of Kansas City, 1972), 197.

TWO

Wesleyan Salvation as Sacramental and Ecclesial

John and Charles Wesley came from a devoted Christian home. Randy Maddox notes that the Wesley brothers' passion for the sacraments as a means of grace never waned. However, one can trace different points of emphasis that resulted in some shift of thinking and preaching. John Wesley was "taught from infancy to reverence the early or 'primitive' church as a model for doctrine, practice, and moral ideals."[1] This reverence followed him into his studies at Oxford.

Part of the Wesleys' pastoral passion was rooted in their own healing and transformation. During their time at Oxford, a group of students began meeting with John and Charles regularly for study and reflection. In the fall of 1730, this group of friends went to the Oxford castle prison to offer food and pastoral care. These acts of compassion grew to include visiting the homebound and poor to share spiritual encouragement, fellowship, and food. This rhythm of compassion connected to rigorous study grounded the regular practices of this group. Their regular, consistent,

---

1. Randy L. Maddox, "Introduction to Wesley's Treatises on the Theology and Practice of Baptism," *The Bicentennial Edition of the Works of John Wesley, Vol. 14: Doctrinal and Controversial Treatises III*, eds Sarah Lancaster, Randy L. Maddox, Kelly Diehl Yates (Nashville: Abingdon Press, 2022), 1. All subsequent references to *The Works of John Wesley* are from the *Bicentennial Edition*, unless otherwise noted.

disciplined actions led others to mock the group by calling them the "Holy Club." Other names of derision followed.[2]

The actions of compassion connected to the practices of soaking in Scripture, prayer, and attending to the sacraments. All were grounded in John Wesley's commitment to live into the gift of "holiness of heart and life."[3] John's reading of William Law's *Serious Call to a Devout and Holy Life* powerfully convinced him of the rich depth of entire consecration to God. Inspired by this reading and Bishop Taylor's *Rules and Exercises of Holy Living and Dying*, Thomas à Kempis's *Christian Pattern*, and others, John writes "of the absolute impossibility of being half a Christian; and I determined through his grace (the absolute necessity of which I was deeply sensible of), to be all devoted to God, to give him all my soul, my body, and my substance."[4] Practices moved to habituated routines of fasting, prayer, Scripture reading, and attending to the sacraments. All these practices formed and shaped one's devotion and sincerity in seeking after **Christian perfection** as the full devotion of maturing in love. It is noteworthy that these habituated practices were joined with acts of compassion from the very beginning. This is the foundation of a **martyr ecclesiology** in the Wesleyan tradition.

---

2. Richard P. Heitzenrater, *Wesley and the People Called Methodists* (Nashville: Abingdon Press, 1995), 42.

3. Heitzenrater, *Wesley and the People Called Methodists*, 43. Heitzenrater suggests that such pursuits honestly sought meaning and transformation but that they also created a burden of duty that attempted to experience assurance through works. This all should be connected to Wesley's travels to the American Colonies, his ultimate failure, and the powerful, *strangely warmed* Aldersgate encounter.

4. John Wesley, *A Plain Account of Christian Perfection: as believed and taught by the Reverend Mr. John Wesley from the year 1725 to 1777*, Reprinted from the complete original text as authorized by the Wesley Conference Office in London, England, 1872, (Kansas City, MO: Beacon Hill Press, 1966), p. 10-11. See ¶ 2-4.

Wesleyan Sacramental Theology

Our ongoing healing in love is always grounded in God's grace. We can never earn or achieve the healing God seeks to offer. However, as the fruit of God's love, these works of piety are to be specifically connected to works of mercy. Such devotion is always doxological in thanksgiving for all that God has done and is doing.

Also in this time John became influenced by the work of several non-jurors[5] who further encouraged so-called primitive practices.[6] These influences encouraged John to insist on immersion in baptism, along with strong affirmations of infant baptism and denying access to the Lord's Table to any who were not baptized (and even denying some who did not receive a triune immersion—immersion three times in the name of Father, Son, and Holy Spirit). However, after his failed ministry in Georgia, Wesley expanded beyond his non-juror and primitive passions.

Upon returning to England, "Wesley was drawn into the emerging evangelical revival, with its pietist focus on the *heart*—emphasizing particularly: authentic *personal* repentance, witnessed by an affective *experience* of God's pardoning love, and issuing in a real *conversion* of one's dispositions and life (the fruit of the Spirit.)"[7] Wesley still celebrated the importance of the sacraments but also began to emphasize the need for a personal response to God's healing invitations. The Moravian influence on John in 1738 convinced him that even with *constant* and *proper* participation in all the sacraments, a human response of faith as a deep trust and confidence in God was necessary for a full unleashing of healing and deep fruitfulness of the sacraments. This faith was more than a mental assent to propositions but a "sure trust and confidence in God that through the merits of Christ my sins are forgiven and I am reconciled to the favour of God."[8]

---

5. Non-jurors in seventeenth-century England were bishops and clergymen who refused to swear allegiance to the monarchs William and Mary; non-jurors were removed from their positions in the Church of England in 1689.

6. Maddox, "Introduction to Wesley's Treatises," *Doctrinal and Controversial Treatises III*, 241.

7. Maddox, "Introduction to Wesley's Treatises, *Doctrinal and Controversial Treatises III*, 244.

8. Maddox, "Introduction to Wesley's Treatises, *Doctrinal and Controversial Treatises III*, 244.

In this season, John Wesley also had his famous Aldersgate experience on May 24, 1738. This experience was a culmination of several building tensions and events in his life. He had recently returned from ministry and personal-life failures in Georgia. John's heart was, as he himself has put it, "strangely warmed" by the Spirit during a reading of Martin Luther's preface to Romans. Wesley experienced a well-spring of faith and conviction of God's assurance that he was loved and valued for who he was in Christ and not for any type of moral or religious work or duty. John felt God's love overwhelm him in a way he had not previously experienced. Considering this deep assurance, John became convinced that God was inviting persons to a deep healing in holy love. While our actions can never save us, they do testify to the fruit of God's love that seeks to flourish within us. A Wesleyan notion of salvation is a healing into *perfect love*, whereby God's love continues to overwhelm and undo the remnants of sin in one's life. The sacraments played a powerful role in this work the Wesleys felt called by God to undertake.

John and Charles had observed that many in England were not experiencing the great hope, freedom, and victorious love of the Christian faith. Part of the intensity of the Wesleys' disciplined devotion was fueled by their frustration with the general nominalism of eighteenth-century faith in Great Britain. While most had been baptized as infants, many were not living a daily, vital faith of love. Furthermore, while disciplined devotion was not the foundation of assurance, it became the fruit that sprang from a deep knowledge of God's love. John's own search for and discovery of assurance shaped his pastoral ministry and sacramental passion. This sacramental passion celebrated a robust participation in the sacraments that included an active, faithful response to the healing offered by God's presence.

While the Moravian influence emphasized the importance of faith as part of a sacramental flourishing, John Wesley eventually parted ways with the Moravians because they encouraged persons not to partake of the means of grace until they had an assurance of faith. Conversely, Wesley understood that the sacraments could be an occasion to help *bolster* one's faith and assurance. As such, Wesley often warned persons of desiring "'the end without the means' i.e., of hoping for growth in faith and holiness without regular participation in the means through which God has chosen to convey grace."[9] This passion for regular attendance to the sacraments coupled with a dynamic faithful response to the healing God offers became the dominant pastoral passion for Wesley throughout his ministry.

Sacramental Revival

As the Wesleyan revival movement took root, the centrality of communal worship in the ministry of preaching and the sacraments grounded the early Methodists. While John and Charles's commitment to the sacraments was not new, their rigorous sacramental discipline was the deep aroma of the Wesleyan revival. As such, the Wesleyan revival can be properly named a *sacramental* revival. The next three chapters will briefly explore how the sacraments were central in the Wesley's *ordo salutis* ("way of salvation"). The sacraments are dynamic occasions of God's *preventing, justifying,* and *sanctifying* grace. While each of these terms has a unique note to play in the orchestra of God's salvation, they should always be seen as existing together in harmony in the full concerto God is working within each person as part of creation's redemption.

---

9. Maddox, "Introduction to Wesley's Treatises, *Doctrinal and Controversial Treatises III,* 244–45.

Sacraments as Occasions of Ongoing Healing and Salvation

Wesleyan historian Ole Borgen notes that the sacraments were a means of "dispensing salvation to [humanity]. Thus, God's grace is considered as bestowed within this frame of reference, to each according to [their] need and situation, expressed in terms of prevenient, convincing, justifying and sanctifying grace."[10] Borgen asserts that, for the Wesleys, growth in holy Christlikeness primarily occurs by God's action through the sacraments: "The means of grace (and thus also the sacraments) are the *ordinary* channels whereby God conveys his grace to [humanity]. Consequently, the means of grace (including baptism and the Lord's Supper) function only within the soteriological framework of the *ordo salutis* and must only be treated systematically with this structural frame."[11] John Wesley asserted that the sacraments play a vital role in both dynamic crisis moments of faith as well as the ongoing maturing in Christlikeness.

When Wesley speaks about the therapeutic healing of God in sanctification—the process of renewing persons into the *imago Dei* (the image of God)—he speaks about salvation in relational categories: love for God, love for others, and caring for creation as additional expression of love. This language describes a person's journey in maturing Christlikeness and holiness.[12]

In the sermon "On Working Out Our Own Salvation," Wesley reflects on the journey of faith and healing that

---

10. Ole E. Borgen, *John Wesley on the Sacraments: A Theological Study* (Grand Rapids: Francis Asbury Press, 1985), 46.

11. Borgen, *John Wesley on the Sacraments*, 46.

12. Wesley, "Sermon 83: On Patience," *The Works of John Wesley, Vol. 3*, ed. Albert C. Outler (Nashville: Abingdon Press, 1976), 174–76, §10; see also Wesley, "Sermon 40: Christian Perfection," 3:104–05, §I.9.

occurs in the lives of all believers and the important role of a response to God's invitation to life:

> . . . If God "worketh in you," then "work out your own salvation." The original word rendered, "work out" implies the doing a thing thoroughly. "Your own"—for you yourselves must do this, or it will be left undone for ever. "Your own salvation"—salvation begins with what is usually termed (and very properly) "preventing grace;" including the first wish to please God, the first dawn of light concerning his will, and the first slight, transient conviction of having sinned against him. All these imply some tendency toward life, some degree of salvation, the beginning of a deliverance from a blind, unfeeling heart, quite insensible of God and the things of God. Salvation is carried on by "convincing grace," usually in Scripture termed "repentance," which brings a larger measure of self-knowledge, and a farther deliverance from the heart of stone. Afterward we experience the proper Christian salvation, whereby "through grace" we "are saved by faith," consisting of those two grand branches, justification and sanctification. By justification we are saved from the guilt of sin, and restored to the favour of God: by sanctification we are saved from the power and root of sin, and restored to the image of God.[13]

Can you hear the full concerto of God's ongoing healing in the life of Christians? The charge to *work out our own salvation* (Philippians 2:12) articulates the importance of a co-operant response to God's healing initiatives. Although God always moves first, God's gracious movement toward creation also empowers creation's response along the way.

---

13. Wesley, "Sermon 85: On Working Out Our Own Salvation," *Works of John Wesley*, 3:203–04, §II.1. This sermon is a bold example of the strong individualism that perhaps plagues the development of a healthy ecclesiology in the Wesleyan tradition.

While affirming the dynamic gift of healing through the Spirit, the question ceases to be "whether we are 'worthy' to receive this gracious empowerment, but whether we co-operantly receive—or squander—its healing potential."[14]

The Means of Grace within the *Ordo Salutis*

If salvation is the healing of the disease of sin, what specific role do the means of grace play in the *ordo salutis*? For Wesley, they are central:

> By "means of grace" I understand outward signs, words, or actions ordained of God, and appointed for this end—to be the ordinary channels whereby he might convey to men preventing, justifying, or sanctifying grace. . . . The chief of these means are prayer, whether in secret or with the great congregation; searching the Scriptures (which implies reading, hearing, and meditating thereon) and receiving the Lord's Supper, eating bread and drinking wine in remembrance of him; and these we believe to be ordained of God as the ordinary channels of conveying his grace to the souls of [humans].[15]

---

14. Maddox, *Responsible Grace*, 198.

15. Wesley, "Sermon 16: The Means of Grace," *Works*, 1:381, §II.1. Wesley also affirms that this is precisely the Church of England's teaching and doctrine. It is noteworthy that prayer, Scripture, and the Lord's Supper are called the chief means of grace for the offering of salvation through preventing, justifying, or sanctifying grace. Ole Borgen asserts that, although Scripture is important, the Lord's Supper is the *primary* means of grace: "The Word plays an important role in God's plan of salvation. But for Wesley, the Lord's Supper always remains the means of grace *par excellence*" (*John Wesley on the Sacraments*, 75). Later in the sermon "The Means of Grace," Wesley elaborates further: "Thirdly, all who desire an increase of the grace of God are to wait for it in partaking of the Lord's Supper" (§III.11). See also "Sermon 101: The Duty of Constant Communion," §I:1: "A second reason every Christian should [receive the Lord's Supper] as often as [they] can is that the benefits of doing it are so great to all that do it in obedience to him; namely, the forgiveness of our past sins and the present strengthening and refreshing of our souls."

A sacrament, more than simply pointing to an experience or spiritual state already accomplished, is itself an event of grace, a transforming, sanctifying event. The sacraments are means of grace that can be properly discussed only under the *ordo salutis.*

As Anglicans, the Wesleys found the ordinary sacramental encounters within the *ordo* and *via salutis* fairly simple. God brings a person into the church through infant baptism, which is the chief symbol of God's **prevenient grace**.[16] At some point, individuals respond to the growing realization through prevenient grace that they are sinners; along with the awareness of need, healing also presents itself. God provides justification, forgiveness, and healing through Jesus Christ.

At a believer's baptism, initial justifying grace is offered as the response to the Spirit's invitation, with **confession** and **repentance**. This initial justifying grace is also offered at infant baptism and seeks and empowers that response all along the way. This justifying grace celebrates both pardon-forgiveness and the **new birth**, also called by Wesley **initial sanctification**. As we grow in faith, we are invited to the Table to partake of the sacrament of the **Lord's Supper**. Although we are baptized only once, we come to the Lord's Supper as often as God makes possible. The Lord's Supper should be considered the *ordinary* and *primary* means by which persons grow in love for God and neighbor; thus, it is the sacrament of sanctification.

______

16. For Wesley, prevenient grace is not *offered* at infant baptism but is a great picture of the church *living in* the gift of prevenient grace. Prevenient grace affirms that persons do not come to God on their own and that God will not give up and has not given up on anyone. It is the idea that *all* persons are preveniently graced by God, which calls into question what precisely infant baptism really does. Wesley is inconsistent but eventually rejects the idea that infant baptism can be directly equated with the new birth.

However, Wesley stated that God offers grace and healing according to need:

> (1) . . . The Lord's Supper was ordained by God to be a means of conveying to [humanity] either preventing or justifying, or sanctifying grace, according to their several necessities. . . . (3) that inasmuch as we come to his Table, not to give him anything but to receive whatsoever he sees best for us, there is no previous preparation indispensably necessary, but a desire to receive whatsoever he pleases to give.[17]

Wesley's teaching that God may offer preventing and justifying grace in addition to sanctifying grace in the Lord's Supper might seem an overreach for many contemporary evangelical Wesleyans who have neglected Wesley's dynamic sacramental theology and practice. However, it demonstrates the significance Wesley placed on the sacraments within the *ordo salutis*, with some important provisions and exceptions.

Within the *ordo salutis*, while the sacraments offer opportunities for healing, they also empower the Christian's response to allow this healing to flourish. Wesley affirmed the means of grace as "exercises that nourish the grace given to us."[18] Hence, the sacraments offer not only grace that must be responded to but also the grace of empowerment *to* respond. Significantly, the sacraments are the *ordinary* means of healing, yet they are not the *only* events of healing transformation.

The designations of *preventing, justifying,* and *sanctifying* grace are not modes of faith but movements of God's performative healing in love. Wesley claimed that God works in the seeking, penitent heart at every stage of faith develop-

---

17. Wesley, "June 28, 1740," Journal 4, *Works of John Wesley: Journal and Diaries II (1738–1743)*, ed. W. Reginald Ward and Richard P. Heitzenrater, 19:159.

18. Maddox, *Responsible Grace*, 201.

ment and growth. The next chapters are meant to offer a rich tapestry of how the sacraments play a central role in both the healing of persons in love but also in reforming and renewing individuals into the church as the body of the crucified and resurrected Christ. While there is no precise formula or process for each person's journey, the church has offered the gospel narrative within a general rhythm.

The very first desire to please God and recognize that we are sinners results from God's *preventing* (prevenient) grace. God's *convincing* grace moves us to confess our sins, seeking forgiveness and transformation. We come to the waters of baptism in response to God's wooing, confessing and repenting of our sin, seeking forgiveness and pardon. This healing is not primarily individual but ecclesial as forgiveness and pardon include initiation into the church. At baptism, we are justified by God and begin the process of *sanctification*. The Lord's Supper is the meal of the baptized to renew the baptismal covenant, while also assisting in our ongoing healing in sanctification. Sanctification is the process of being healed from the power of sin to be restored to the image of God to love. As we have been loved by God, God empowers us to love God, ourselves, others, and creation. We can and *must* love.

In an ordinary sense, baptism is a sacrament of justification while the Lord's Supper is a sacrament of ongoing sanctification. Within this regular and ordinary gospel journey, the Wesleys also celebrate the ways God can heal in extra-ordinary ways in the sacraments according to the need of each person and community. This ability demonstrates the goodness of God and the dynamic power of the sacramental encounter.

THREE

Wesleyan Prevenient Grace

Prevenient grace—or preventing grace (Wesley used the terms interchangeably)— within Wesleyanism affirms four things. First, God is the main actor who initiates, empowers, and sustains all things working toward the salvation and redemption of creation. Although humanity needs redemption, the "initiative and cause of our salvation is God alone, more specifically in God's love . . . thus [Wesley's] insistence upon the doctrine of the Trinity . . . the involvement of the full Godhead, Father, Son, and Holy Spirit, in the work of salvation."[1] God alone heals the disease of sin. "It is God who works, and [humans] who receive and respond, *after God in his grace has made this possible.*"[2] Borgen asserts that only in God's initiative and sustaining activity do the sacraments bring about soteriological healing.

Second, Wesley understands prevenient grace as "to go or come before," enabling all responses to God.[3] God's prevenient grace forms the core of all Wesleyan **soteriology**. The claim that God offers prevenient grace in the waters of baptism or through the Lord's Supper might imply that prevenient grace comes only to those who have been baptized

---

1. Borgen, *John Wesley on the Sacraments*, 83.

2. Borgen, *John Wesley on the Sacraments*, 83. This is a crucial element of Wesley's soteriological methodology.

3. See Wesley, "Sermon 43: The Scripture Way of Salvation," *Works of John Wesley*, 2:163, § III.2.

or commune at the Table, but prevenient grace is offered to all and comes at other times outside the sacraments as well.

Third, prevenient grace speaks directly to the belief of universal atonement that distinguishes Wesley from the Synod of Dort's belief of limited atonement for the elect. Affirming universal atonement does not mean all persons will be saved regardless of their response to God. It simply means all persons have the possibility of being saved (1 Timothy 2:4; 2 Peter 3:9). Later in Wesley's career, in debates with Calvinist predestinarians about the universality of atonement, Wesley "ultimately declared that any inherited human guilt was universally cancelled *at birth*, as one benefit of Christ's redemption. In effect, his concession of inherited guilt was now annulled by the invocation of prevenient grace."[4] Prevenient grace describes God's *coming before* to all persons, that *all* may find life.[5]

In the gift of conscience, Wesley affirms that God reaches out to all, seeking to draw us into healing so that we may love God, love others, and care for creation. Wesley describes the connection between prevenient grace and conscience:

> This faculty seems to be what is usually meant by those who speak of "natural conscience," an expression frequently found in some of our best authors, but yet not strictly just. For though in one sense it may be termed "natural," because it is found in all, yet properly speaking it is not natural; but a supernatural gift of God, above all his natural endowments. No, it is not

---

4. Maddox, *Responsible Grace*, 75. Maddox references Wesley's Letter to John Mason of November 21, 1776 in John Telford, ed., *The Letters of the Rev. John Wesley* (London: Epworth, 1931), 6:239–40. Cf. "Sermon 59: God's Love to Fallen Man," *Works of John Wesley*, 2:434, §II.14.

5. Distinct from the Reformed tradition, Wesley also affirms that God's healing salvation is for all and not simply for the elect, as some restricted predestined group. Prevenient grace is the foundation for the belief within Wesley of universal atonement, offered to all who would respond.

Wesleyan Sacramental Theology

Protestants have named baptism and the Lord's Supper as sacraments because of their explicit divine command in Scripture. However, God certainly offers healing and transformation well beyond these two practices in communal worship. God can offer individual and ecclesial healing at any time and place because creation is infused with God's presence—hence, we live in a sacramental world. Sacramental moments are grounded in the universal gift of prevenient grace.

nature but the Son of God that is "the true light, which enlighteneth every [person] which cometh into the world." So that we may say to every human creature, "He," not nature, "hath shown thee, O man, what is good." And it is his Spirit who giveth thee an inward check, who causeth thee to feel uneasy, when thou walkest in any instance contrary to the light which he hath given thee.[6]

Wesley is not denying the importance of a person's response to God but asserting that the very awareness of human sinfulness coming through our conscience is a gift of God's prevenient grace.[7] Randy Maddox suggests that one function of prevenient grace is that it leads to *awakening*.

Fourth, Wesley affirmed (contra Calvinism and Lutheranism) that the gift of prevenient grace denies the inevitability of sin. The classic Wesleyan text declares: "No man sins because he has not grace, but because he does not use the grace which he hath."[8] This text offers important implications for the sacraments of baptism and the Lord's Supper as a means of grace. God's healing presence in the sacraments empowers persons to live out the healing offered by God. While sin is a terrible disease, Wesley affirms that, as Christians are healed in love, love should become more and more the habitual response as sin becomes accidental. Through Christ, God makes it possible for us to choose love as we respond to God's healing presence.

---

6. Wesley, "Sermon 105: On Conscience," *Works of John Wesley*, 3:482, §I.5.

7. Maddox, *Responsible Grace*, 160–61.

8. Wesley, "Sermon 85: On Working Out Our Own Salvation," *Works of John Wesley*, 3:207, §III.4.

Sacramental and Ecclesial Implications of Prevenient Grace

Let's consider four sacramental and ecclesial implications of prevenient grace. First, prevenient grace rejects Pelagianism. Pelagius has often been charged with asserting that persons can come to God and choose love over sin *on their own effort*, without God's assistance. Wesleyans reject that idea and proclaim that God alone initiates faith, while also sustaining and empowering the church. In sacramental practice, the church must never conceive of its celebrations of baptism or the Lord's Supper as meritorious acts but as actions in response to God. Infant baptism is a great symbol of prevenient grace because it demonstrates the way that God moves before any full, embodied, personal response is even possible. Acknowledging the prevenient grace that is present in sacraments like baptism does not mean that those who are not baptized have not or could not receive God's wooing, preventing work.

Second, prevenient grace reminds the church that God works in all the world. Therefore, the church's posture toward the world must never support a **sacred-secular dualism**.[9] This position strongly rebukes any in the church who claim that the world (including persons in it) is evil, or to be feared or avoided. The entire world—including all humans—is sacred because of God's creating and sustaining presence in it. Rather than disdaining or fearing the world, God's prevenient grace in the world compels the church in hope to go into the entire world participating in God's further bringing of the kingdom of God to earth as it is in heaven—from sin to love.

---

9. For a fuller discussion of sacred-secular dualism and how it relates to the church, see Brent D. Peterson, "Rejecting Dualism and Empire," *The Wesleyan Theology Series: The Church* (Kansas City, MO: The Foundry Publishing, 2023), 161–74.

Third, prevenient grace reminds the church that the church does not bring God to the world. The church, which comes in the light of Christ by the power of the Spirit, brings hope as well as illuminates God's already-present light.

Fourth, even though God offers prevenient grace to all, Wesley affirms that both baptism and the Lord's Supper are important means of grace that reinforce our awareness of our sin, removing apathy, and empowering our initial moves toward life and love that hopefully will lead us to convincing grace and on to justifying grace. Even the devout Christian of fifty years and beyond can find occasion at the Lord's Supper to be reminded that God loves her, that God desires her to be set free from sin, and thus encounter in a powerful way afresh and anew God's prevenient grace.

In spiritual formation and discipleship, the journey of life—though not intended to be chaotic—is not simply linear but spiritually dynamic. God continues to encounter us where we are, inviting us both personally and ecclesially into deeper levels of healing in love.

FOUR

Wesleyan Justifying Grace

The second aspect of Wesley's *ordo salutis* is justifying grace. As prevenient grace awakens us to our sinfulness and need for forgiveness, it also opens us up to the remedy. *Convincing grace*, or *repentance*, leads a person toward conversion and justifying grace. Coming forward penitently in faith is a proper response to God's prevenient and convincing grace at the waters of baptism and on occasion at the Table, where persons may experience God's justifying grace. Wesley suggests that justifying grace offers pardon, forgiveness, and assurance.[1] It is the regular and *ordinary* story of Christianity that this pardon, forgiveness, and assurance are most profoundly offered at baptism, inviting the God-empowered human response of conversion.

Within a Wesleyan soteriology, the gifts of God's grace are not restricted only to the moment of baptism, given definitively once and then never again. Wesleyans can agree with the tradition that justifying grace *is* offered at baptism, but we also suggest that it can be refreshed and deepened along the journey. These gifts of God are ongoing and continue to minister as we grow and mature in Christlikeness. Wesley considered how our *initial justification* elicits and launches the healing of initial sanctification in the new birth. Moreover, Wesley resisted the idea that salvation is

---

1. See Wesley, "Sermon 101: The Duty of Constant Communion," *Works of John Wesley*, 3:442–43, §I:2–3.

limited to imputed righteousness. God seeks not only to *declare* persons righteous (imputed righteousness) but also to *make* them righteous (sanctification).[2]

In affirming the healing of sanctifying grace, Wesley distinguished both *initial* and *final* justification. Initial justification is fully salvific; it testifies to God's pardoning love for us. Initial justification (like initial sanctification) also activates "our deliverance from the power as well as the guilt of sin."[3] Yet God offers more healing as we respond to this work of pardon. Initial justification opens the door to our response within the healing of sanctification, and this growth of healing in sanctification can make possible our final justification. The celebration of our final justification should be connected to Wesley's understanding of glorification. Maddox sums up the key Wesleyan soteriological distinctive: "God's *gracious* empowering acceptance [justification] enhances rather than replaces our responsive and *responsible* growth in holiness."[4] Justification paves the road to the fuller healing of sanctification. We are invited to continually respond to God's gracious healing.

The tensions are clear but important. In a Wesleyan celebration of salvation, God is the primary actor offering healing and salvation not based on what humans can achieve. Yet this gift must be responded to for the full healing into the restored likeness of God to occur. The human response is always empowered by God, not a work of achievement. Through and through it is God's grace as the healing, transforming presence of God. Yet in God's providence, the full healing invites, requires, and empowers our participation as an act of joy and thanksgiving for what God has done and is doing. Healing into Christlikeness is

---

2. Maddox, *Responsible Grace*, 167.

3. Maddox, *Responsible Grace*, 171.

4. Maddox, *Responsible Grace*, 172.

contingent upon God's pardoning and prevenient grace. The fullness of God's acceptance in final justification is contingent upon our responsive participation in the healing of sanctification. "Justification is not the stage we leave behind to enter sanctification; it is a facet of God's saving grace permeating the entire Way of Salvation."[5] Within all this precise technical theological language, the invitation is clear. God desires that all be saved. God has pardoned and canceled sin for all. Yet, to allow this full, gracious healing to flourish and live, we must continually respond (empowered by God) to God's healing into holy love.

These considerations raise an important caution. Both the older and younger son in Luke 15 forgot what it meant to *be* a son. They both stopped responding to the father's gracious generosity of life and both saw their sonship slipping away. Ergo, they were both prodigals. Too often we Christians fail to remember God's transforming work and anointing at baptism and the lifelong message of good news. Hence, there are also occasions when God's assurance and forgiveness declared at baptism are encountered and experienced again at the Lord's Supper. Later, we will connect this concept to the conversation celebrating the Lord's Supper as a meal of the baptized—an occasion to confirm one's baptismal covenant. In this way the Lord's Supper both reminds and renews and empowers the ongoing, vibrant baptismal covenant: *Remember whose you are!*

Ole Borgen concludes that "since justification means forgiveness of sins and finding favour before God, it must follow that the Lord's Supper is also a converting ordinance."[6] Wesley responds directly to those who disallow the notion of the Lord's Supper as offering converting grace:

---

5. Maddox, *Responsible Grace*, 172.

6. Borgen, "No End without the Means: John Wesley and the Sacraments," *Asbury Theological Journal* 46, No. 1 (1991), 79.

46

Wesleyan Sacramental Theology

One unique, though somewhat controversial, aspect of a WST is the notion that the Lord's Supper can be understood as a converting ordinance.

Many have affirmed that the Lord's Supper is not a converting, but a confirming ordinance. And among us it has been diligently taught that none but those who are converted, who "have received the Holy Ghost" who are believers in the full sense, ought to communicate. But experience shows the gross falsehood of that assertion that the Lord's Supper is not a converting ordinance. Ye are the witnesses. For many now present know, the very beginning of your conversion to God (perhaps, in some, the first deep conviction) was wrought at the Lord's Supper. Now one single instance of this kind overthrows that whole assertion.[7]

The Lord's Supper can be both a converting *and* confirming ordinance. As a converting ordinance, God offers justifying grace, pardon, and forgiveness to the one who comes penitently seeking healing. As part of the gift of justifying grace, God also offers a confirming grace where we can receive assurance that our conversion is true. Like Paul says in Romans 8:16, the Spirit will testify with our spirit that we are children of God.

Therefore, as justifying grace offers pardon, forgiveness, and healing through the church, God invites sinners to the Table. Charles Wesley's poetry affirms this sentiment in the 1747 hymn "Come, Sinners, to the Gospel Feast," as well as in his and his brother's compiled *Hymns on the Lord's Supper*.

> *Lord, I have now invited all:*
> *And instant still the guests shall call,*
> *Still shall I all invite to thee:*
> *For O my God, it seems but right*
> *In mine, thy meanest servant's sight,*
> *That where all is there all should be.*[8]

---

7. Wesley, "June 27, 1740," *Works of John Wesley: Journal and Diaries II*, 19:158.

8. John Wesley and Charles Wesley, "Hymn IX," *Hymns on the Lord's Supper* (Bristol, UK: Felix Farley, 1747). See also "Hymn LX," stanza 2.

All are invited to come repentantly, seeking pardon and forgiveness.

Justifying grace also offers the gift of assurance. John Wesley came to believe that, although justifying grace is more ordinarily first experienced at baptism, a person can receive further assurance of faith through the Lord's Supper: "I then indeed found one who, when many (according to their custom) laboured to persuade her she had no faith, replied, with a spirit they were not able to resist, 'I know that "the life which I now live, I live by faith in the Son of God, who loved me, and gave himself for me." And he has never left me one moment, since the hour he was made known to me in the breaking of bread.'"[9] Wesley asserts from this testimony that the assurance of faith can come through the Lord's Supper:

> What is to be inferred from this undeniable matter of fact—one that had not faith received it in the Lord's Supper? Why, (1) that there are "means of grace," i.e., outward ordinances, whereby the inward grace of God is ordinarily conveyed to [humans], whereby the faith that brings salvation is conveyed to them who before had it not; (2) that one of these means is the Lord's Supper; and (3) that he who has not this faith ought to wait for it in the use both of this and of the other means which God hath ordained.[10]

This does not imply that Wesley let those who were unbaptized come to the Table, nor did he allow those in poor standing with the class meetings to do so.[11] It is important to offer a historical reminder: The sinners Wesley welcomed

---

9. Wesley, "November 7, 1739," Journal 4, *Works of John Wesley*, 19:120–21.

10. Wesley, "November 7, 1739," *Works of John Wesley*, 19:121.

11. Regular participation in the bands and class meetings was of such importance to Wesley that failure to attend was considered to symbolize one's lack of desire to be transformed in the image of God. Tickets were often issued at the meetings for entrance into worship and the celebration of Communion.

to the Table were *baptized* sinners. In eighteenth-century England, most people were baptized as infants.

God may offer a strengthening, deepening, assuring faith at the Table to those who have felt as if they had none. In one of the *Hymns on the Lord's Supper*, this pardon and assurance are described as seeing and encountering the crucified Christ.

> *See the slaughter'd sacrifice,*
> *See the altar stain'd with blood!*
> *Crucified before our eyes*
> *Faith discerns the dying God,*
> *Dying that our souls might live,*
> *Gasping at his death, forgive!*[12]

More than simple observation, this seeing is a transforming encounter with the crucified yet resurrected Savior. The idea that seeing Christ is a healing, forgiving encounter emphasizes the importance of Christ's presence in both the Lord's Supper and the cleansing waters of baptism.

Gift of Assurance

Offering the gift of assurance is a key facet of the *ordo salutis* in the soteriological renewing of persons into the likeness and image of God. In light of the revival, Wesley became convinced that assurance was connected to justification.[13] Therefore, Wesley did permit those who did not have the gift of assurance to come to the Table with the hope they might receive it there.

Although Wesley did allow the possibility that God could use the Lord's Supper as a converting ordinance with the gift of justifying grace, this is not the ordinary *ordo salutis*. The Lord's Supper as a converting ordinance should

---

12. Wesley and Wesley, "Hymn XVIII," *Hymns on the Lord's Supper.*

13. Richard Heitzenrater, "An Introductory Comment—Sermons 18–19," *Works of John Wesley,* 1:416.

be understood as the exception, not the rule. Connected to the notion of the Lord's Supper as a converting ordinance is the conversation about what it means to *fence the table*, which we will explore more fully in the chapter on faithful eucharistic practices.

Sacramental and Ecclesial Implications of Justifying Grace

First, faithful Wesleyan practice invites all persons to come penitently into the waters of baptism and to the Table. The Table must not be restricted only to those who previously have confessed their sins and received Christ's forgiveness but must also be open to those who come humbly seeking God's justifying pardon and forgiveness. Even as baptism is the ordinary means of God's declaration of forgiveness and justification in response to one's confession, the **Eucharist** may also be an occasion of conversion.

Second, it is pastorally appropriate for those with waning faith to come in hope to the Table, that they may experience again the love, peace, and forgiveness of God. The Table is not only for those who *feel* justified, pardoned, and loved; coming to the Table may be an occasion when persons encounter the Spirit's testimony of assurance that they are children of God (see Romans 8:16). Even as the power of God's justifying grace is divinely given, the Lord's Supper can be a renewed encounter with God's declaration of pardon, forgiveness, and assurance first pronounced at baptism—which can be especially meaningful for those baptized as infants with no memory of their baptism, or those whose baptism is now so long ago their memory of their assurance has faded.

Third, in both baptism and the Lord's Supper, encountering Christ's presence becomes the event of pardon, forgiveness, and assurance. This affirmation is not simply a disembodied proclamation for mental assent. In both sacraments, persons are forgiven, healed, and transformed through an encounter with the crucified and resurrected Christ, by the power of the Spirit, by the will of the Father. It is not that God needs to do supplemental work at the Lord's Supper after the justifying and forgiving work done in baptism. Rather, for many on the human journey, persons need to again encounter and experience not simply a reminder of God's past forgiveness but also a renewed declaration by God that one is loved, forgiven, pardoned, and seen.

Fourth, although God can offer justifying grace at the Table, that is not the ordinary *ordo salutis*. In the Wesleyan tradition, the Lord's Supper should principally be considered the sacrament of sanctification—a confirming ordinance.

FIVE

Wesleyan Sanctifying Grace

Because God seeks and woos creation all along the way, responses to God's sanctifying healing are the full aim of the *ordo salutis* in the Wesleyan tradition.[1] Justification and sanctification are the two performative actions in the forgiving and healing of Christians by God as part of the local body. Care should be given in how we proclaim and embody God's salvation as healing to love, since precision in language can lead to more faithful sacramental practice and Christian formation.

New Birth: Initial Sanctification

The new birth plays an important role in Wesley's *ordo salutis*. Even though justification and the new birth occur at the same time, they have distinct meanings in relation to salvation:

> But though it be allowed that justification and the new birth are in point of time inseparable from each other, yet are they easily distinguished as being not the same, but things of a widely different nature. Justification implies only a relative, the new birth a

---

1. Sanctification does not undermine the importance of repentance in justifying grace. If we are not careful, our discussions of sanctification may make it seem as if justification is not quite good enough. This should not be affirmed. However, it is Wesley's strong belief that God desires *more* than justification. The call to love and to holiness seeks to woo persons in the church to deeper maturity and perfection in love.

real, change. God in justifying us does something *for*
us: in begetting us again he does the work *in* us. The
former changes our outward relation to God, so that of
enemies we become children; by the latter our inmost
souls are changed, so that of sinners we become saints.
The one restores us to the *favour*, the other to the *image*
of God. The one is the taking away the *guilt*, the other
the taking away the *power*, of sin. So that although
they are joined together in point of time, yet are they
of wholly distinct natures.[2]

The new birth occurs at conversion in initial sanctification.
Justification emphasizes God's juridical (or "legal") forgiveness, while the new birth emphasizes God's healing and
cleansing as we are renewed in the likeness and image of
God to holy love.

John Wesley affirmed that new birth was the means
by which persons are *born again*, which is a healing and
growth in holiness. In his sermon on the new birth he affirms the great gift of holiness:

Gospel holiness is no less than the image of God
stamped upon the heart; it is no other than the whole
mind which was in Christ Jesus; it consists of all
heavenly affections and tempers mingled together in
one. It implies such a continual, thankful love to him
who hath not withheld from us his Son, his only Son,
as makes it natural, and in a manner necessary to us,
to love every child of man; as fills us "with bowels of
mercies, kindness, gentleness, long-suffering:" It is
such a love of God as teaches us to be blameless in all
manner of conversation; as enables us to present our
souls and bodies, all we are and all we have, all our

---

2. Wesley, "Sermon 19: The Great Privilege of Those That Are Born of God,"
Works of John Wesley, 1:431–32, §2, emphasis added. See also "Sermon 45: The
New Birth," *Works of John Wesley,* 2:186–201.

thoughts, words, and actions, a continual sacrifice to
God, acceptable through Christ Jesus.[3]

Wesley's therapeutic understanding of the *ordo salutis* is
embodied in the gift of sanctification, the healing of being
renewed in the image of God.

Randy Maddox notes that the new birth is the foun-
dational facet of sanctification for Wesley. Maddox asserts
that the new birth "addresses the question of our *ability* for
recovering any holiness in our sin-distorted lives. . . . Any
such ability is *graciously restored*."[4] Maddox reminds us that
Wesley's idea of being born again, or regenerated, had a
wide breadth of meaning, "being inwardly changed by the
almighty operation of the Spirit of God; changed from sin
to holiness, renewed in the image of him who created us."[5]
Maddox also notes that the new birth could be equated
with entire sanctification, and suggests that Charles Wesley
did such but that, after John's Aldersgate experience and his
involvement in the new revivalism, he began to distinguish
the new birth from sanctification—"the first being the
rejuvenation of our human faculties that accompanies the
restored pardoning presence of God in our lives, while the
second is gradual renewal of our moral nature that is then
possible."[6] In other words, the new birth is the beginning
of sanctification. As such, both the new birth and sanctification should be identified with regeneration. "Wesley was
convinced that *both* should be, as increasing *degrees* of a
larger reality."[7] As we respond to God's call for deeper heal-

---

3. Wesley, "Sermon 45: The New Birth," *Works of John Wesley*, 2:194, §III:1.

4. Maddox, *Responsible Grace*, 176.

5. Wesley, *The Doctrine of Original Sin, The Works of John Wesley, Vol. 9, 3rd edition*, ed. Thomas Jackson (reprinted Grand Rapids: Baker, 1979), 308, §II. Hereafter referred to as *Works of John Wesley* (Jackson).

6. Maddox, *Responsible Grace*, 159.

7. Maddox, *Responsible Grace*, 159.

ing, "the new birth commences further co-operant transformation of our lives, empowered by sanctifying grace."[8]

Sanctifying Grace: Ongoing Healing in God

The gift of sanctifying grace has three interconnected yet unique facets.

First, sanctifying grace heals and recreates Christians in the likeness of God.

Second, sanctifying grace celebrates how powerful events and encounters of entire sanctification are also connected to a continual **eschatological** journey of growth and maturity into those dynamic events.

Third, this sanctifying grace seeks to renew and unify believers into the church.

It will be easily observed that more time and space has been given to this chapter on sanctifying grace than was given to preventing and justifying grace. The difference is not a subtle way of elevating the value of one over the others. It is merely an acknowledgment of the reality that both preventing and justifying grace are connected to the beginning of the salvation journey, while sanctifying grace ties in to the long, ongoing maturity that takes place over the rest of one's lifetime. Preventing and justifying grace prepare and make fertile the soil of the long and full healing of sanctifying grace.

#1: Healed and Renewed in the Likeness of God as the Imago Dei

Sanctifying grace emphasizes the continual healing of the sin-disordered tempers and the continual renewal of the image of God in us. Wesley employs the language "circumcision of the heart" in his sermon of the same title to describe sanctification:

---

8. Maddox, *Responsible Grace*, 170.

That habitual disposition of soul which in the Sacred Writings is termed "holiness," and which directly implies the being cleansed from sin, "from all filthiness both of flesh and spirit," and by consequence the being endued with those virtues which were also in Christ Jesus, the being so "renewed in the image of our mind" as to be "perfect, as our Father in heaven is perfect."[9]

Sanctifying grace continues the healing from a disposition of idolatrous self-centeredness to one of love. This renewal in the image of God is a renewal to love God, love self, love others, and care for creation. Wesley further describes how sanctification as renewal in the image of God invites the church to offer itself in praise as a living sacrifice:

And, first, we have known a large number of persons, of every age and sex, from early childhood to extreme old age, who have given all the proofs which the nature of the thing admits that they were "sanctified throughout," "cleansed from all pollution both of flesh and spirit;" that they "loved the Lord their God with all their heart, and mind, and soul, and strength;" that they continually presented their souls and bodies *a living sacrifice, holy, acceptable to God*": in consequence of which they "rejoiced evermore, prayed without ceasing, and in everything gave thanks". And this, and no other, is what we believe to be true, scriptural sanctification.[10]

God continually cleanses those being sanctified. Thinking about Romans 12, those being sanctified respond to this healing by continually presenting themselves as a living sacrifice. It must be observed that this sacrifice is **doxological**—it is done in thanks and praise for what God has done and is doing. The church's doxological offering

---

9. Wesley, "Sermon 17: The Circumcision of the Heart," *Works of John Wesley*, 1:402–03, §I:1.

10. Wesley, "Sermon 86: A Call to Backsliders," *Works of John Wesley*, 3:224–25, §2:3 (4), emphasis added.

of itself as a living sacrifice both *responds to* God's healing and also opens the church to God's continuing perfection in love, making explicit the gift of being renewed into the image of God—a relational renewal in God. This understanding creates a strong link between sanctification and the concept of **theosis**. This healing begins in the waters of baptism and continues to grow and mature through regular participation at the Table.

Sanctification as Theosis

In exploring how sanctification is a renewal in the likeness of God, several Wesley scholars suggest that Wesley's view of sanctification is deeply influenced by the Eastern Orthodox understanding of theosis.[11] Michael J. Christensen defines theosis as deification: "Theosis in the Eastern Orthodox tradition is a vision of human potential for perfection, anticipated in ancient Greece, witnessed to in both the Old and New Testaments, and developed by Patristic Christian theologians of the first five centuries after Christ."[12] This potential of perfection is not an isolated state of ethical supremacy. Rather, theosis is thoroughly relational. Christensen further asserts, "The idea of theosis is that God and humanity progressively achieve a *union* in Christ which in the end both blurs and preserves the distinction between Creator and creation, as in a mirror perfectly reflecting the source of its image."[13] The healing of creatures

---

11. K. Steve McCormick claims that Wesley's notion of theosis is his "most comprehensive response to the question of the nature of the Christian life. . . . It was faith filled with the energy of love." McCormick also claims that this strand of theosis comes "within his own Anglican heritage, a strand borrowed from the Eastern Fathers, most notably John Chrysostom." K. Steve McCormick, "Theosis in Chrysostom and Wesley: An Eastern Paradigm of Faith and Love," *Wesleyan Theological Journal* 26 (1991): 52.

12. Michael J. Christensen, "Theosis and Sanctification: John Wesley's Reformulation of a Patristic Doctrine," *Wesleyan Theological Journal* 31, no. 2 (1996): 72.

13. Christensen, "Theosis and Sanctification," 72.

to be who God created them to be in God's image describes the hope of salvation.

E. Byron Anderson suggests that John Wesley builds upon the Eastern teaching of theosis in fleshing out his understanding of perfection. He says that theosis is the process of "being changed 'from glory to glory' and the character of the Christian life that is 'already but not yet.'"[14] Maddox concurs that theosis fits well within Wesley's understanding of sanctification: "For Wesley, then, the Spirit's work of sanctification was not merely a forensic declaration of how God will treat us. . . . It was a process of character formation that is made possible by a restored participation of fallen humanity in the divine life and power. This understanding of sanctification has significant parallels with the Eastern Orthodox theme of deification (theosis).[15]

Growth in character is growth in the likeness of God, which properly names the gift of sanctification. Similarly, Anderson notes, "theosis is the gradual movement of persons toward the attainment of likeness to God in virtue, wisdom, and knowledge of God."[16] Furthermore, Anderson suggests that divinization is grounded in three theological claims: that "persons are created in the image and likeness of God (Genesis 1:27), that humanity retains in its nature the essential quality of life graced by God, and that, in its freedom, humanity has the potential for losing or attaining a likeness to God. This process of divinization is rooted in the past, ongoing, and future work of God in Jesus Christ through the Holy Spirit."[17]

---

14. E. Byron Anderson, *Worship and Christian Identity: Practicing Ourselves* (Collegeville, MN: Liturgical Press, 2003), 175.

15. Maddox, *Responsible Grace*, 122.

16. Anderson, *Worship and Christian Identity*, 175.

17. Anderson, *Worship and Christian Identity*, 175. Anderson's articulation of divinization aligns itself not only with Wesley's doctrine of sanctification but also that of prevenient grace. Specifically affirming that "humanity retains in its nature the essential quality of life graced by God" speaks against a doctrine

Wesley affirms that God makes us in the image of God. Sanctification is growth in the restored ability to love God, self, and others, and to care for creation more fully. Scholars agree this characterization describes Wesley's understanding of the growth and healing of persons who were created in the *imago dei* to be conformed to his likeness.[18]

Wesley further imagines continual healing in the image of God until glorification—our full restoration into the likeness of God.

> For "if we say that we have fellowship with him, and walk in darkness, we lie, and do not the truth." But by the renewal of our minds in the image of him that created us, we are still more capable of his influences; and by means of a daily intercourse with him, we are more and more transformed into his likeness, till we are satisfied with it.
>
> This likeness to God, this conformity of our will and affections to his will, is, properly speaking, holiness; and to produce this in us, is the proper end and design of all the influences of the Holy Spirit. By means of his presence with us, we receive from him a great fulness of holy virtues; we take such features of resemblance in our spirits as correspond to his original perfections. And thus

---

of original sin where human capacity for God is utterly abolished as a result of the fall. This difference speaks into the important distinction between the *image* and *likeness* of God. In some measure, being "created in the image of God" can be understood as God's prevenient grace that God created us with the capacity to receive and give love. *Likeness* is best understood as glorification—the result of sanctification.

18. While worthy of discussion, this project will not take lengths to separate the distinctions between image and likeness. While Wesley uses "image" more frequently, Anderson's connection to "likeness" is appropriate and enlightening for any discussion on sanctification. Mildred Bangs Wynkoop offers a brief exegetical and theological discussion on their similarities and distinctions in the second edition (2015) of *A Theology of Love*, 124–31. See also Maddox, *Responsible Grace*, 68–70, and H. Ray Dunning, *Grace, Faith & Holiness* (Kansas City, MO: Beacon Hill Press of Kansas City, 1988), 151–60.

we are sealed by him, in the first sense, by way of preparation for our day of redemption.[19]

Created in the image of God, humanity must undergo continual re-creation into the likeness of God as its potential
and goal.[20] Being continually formed into the likeness of
God is holiness.

#2: Perfection as Continual Healing

John Wesley states that his understanding of perfection (what most today call holiness, or sanctification) in
the *ordo salutis* does not mean that one becomes free from
errors, mistakes, or blemishes (the idea behind the Latin
word *perfectum*); instead, perfection consists in humanity
becoming what it is created to be—a people called to love:
"No one then is so perfect in this life as to be free from
ignorance. Nor, secondly, from mistake, which indeed is
almost an unavoidable consequence of it; seeing those who
'know but in part' are ever liable to err touching the things
which they know not."[21] Later in the sermon on Christian
perfection Wesley articulates what this perfection looks
like, illustrating the healing offered:

> Christian perfection therefore does not imply (as some
> . . . seem to have imagined) an exemption either from
> ignorance or mistake, or infirmities or temptations.
> Indeed, it is only another term for holiness. They are
> two names for the same thing. Thus everyone that

---

19. Wesley, "Sermon 138: On Grieving the Holy Spirit," *Works of John Wesley* (Jackson), 7:491, §III.3.

20. See also: "Our first parents did enjoy the presence of the Holy Spirit; for they were created in the image and likeness of God, which was no other than his Spirit. By that he communicates himself to his creatures, and by that alone they can bear any likeness to him. It is, indeed, his life in them; and so properly divine, that, upon this ground, angels and regenerate men are called his children." Wesley, "Sermon 141: On the Holy Spirit," *Works of John Wesley* (Jackson), 7:509, §I.1.

21. Wesley, "Sermon 40: Christian Perfection," *Works of John Wesley,* 1:101–02, §I.4.

is perfect is holy, and everyone that is holy is, in the Scripture sense, perfect. Yet we may, lastly, observe that neither in this respect is there any absolute perfection on earth. There is no "perfection of degrees," as it is termed; none which does not admit of a continual increase. So that how much soever any [person] hath attained, or in how high a degree soever [they are] perfect, [they] hath still need to "grow in grace," and daily to advance in the knowledge and love of God [our] Saviour.[22]

Healing always continues because no absolute perfection on earth occurs; growth in love always increases in this life. Wesley thus implicitly affirms that a Christian's healing to love will not be fully achieved in this life.

Wesley's doctrine of sanctification intersects with his sacramental theology because he considers sanctification to be both an instantaneous event and a gradual process of maturity. Lorna Lock-Nah Khoo writes, "The Wesleys saw the Eucharist as a therapeutic sacrament providing 'the medicine of immortality' for communicants as they seek to be healed of their present condition and become 'perfected in love.'"[23] What begins at justification and the new birth *ordinarily* at baptism continues, "till in another instant the heart is cleansed from all sin, and filled with pure love to God and [humanity]. But even that love increases more and more, till we 'grow up in all things into him that is our head,' 'till we attain the measure of the stature of the fullness of Christ.'"[24] Communing at the Lord's Supper may be the instant when the heart is cleansed from all sin

---

22. Wesley, "Sermon 40: Christian Perfection," *Works of John Wesley,* 1:104–05, §I.9.

23. Lorna Lock-Nah Khoo, *Wesleyan Eucharistic Spirituality: Its Nature, Sources, and Future* (Adelaide, Australia: ATF Press, 2005), 99.

24. Wesley, "Sermon 85: On Working Out Your Own Salvation," *Works of John Wesley,* 3:204, §II.1.

(entire sanctification). Yet Wesley must not be understood as saying that the event becomes a moment of final consummation, or a full and complete healing. As Maddox states, "When one understands sanctification on Wesley's terms, as a lifelong process of healing our sin-distorted affections, there is an obvious need for continually renewing the empowerment for this healing."[25] In the event of entire sanctification, humans **consecrate** themselves and God spiritually transforms, but growth and healing continue in the one who testifies to entire sanctification until glorification—which Wesley affirmed does not happen in this life (if at all).

Being Perfected in Love: An Eschatological Moment and Hope

The continual healing of sanctifying grace occurring in the Eucharist is an eschatological event and becoming. E. Byron Anderson, drawing upon the rich resource of Geoffrey Wainwright's *Eucharist and Eschatology*, suggests, "What is 'already' is provisional; it is *until*. There is more to come. In this sense what is 'already' is 'not yet.'"[26] Anderson presses deeper as to the nature of the "not yet," the teleological creation of humanity by God. Speaking directly of Wesley, Anderson writes, "The experience of salvation in the present life prepares the individual for the life of the kingdom and represents a present realization of that life. The present experience of sanctification, of happiness and holiness, provides an entrance into what remains future, the believer not only living and walking toward eternity but also living 'the life of eternity, the life of love that characterizes the king-

---

25. Maddox, *Responsible Grace*, 202. This healing is precisely what regular participation in the Eucharist offers.

26. Anderson, *Worship and Christian Identity*, 173.

dom of God.'"[27] The sanctifying grace continually offered at the Table exemplifies the process of growth in sanctification, but this growth must never be seen as achievement or personal success; instead, it must be grounded in the continual growth of love for God and neighbor.

Because the Eucharist offers eschatological healing, Wesley could affirm that it is a pledge of the future and final healing that is to come.[28]

O might the sacred word
Set forth our dying Lord,
Point us to thy sufferings past,
Present grace and strength impart,
Give our ravish'd souls a taste,
Pledge of glory in our heart.[29]

Sure pledge of extacies unknown
Shall this divine communion be,
The ray shall rise into a sun,
The drop shall swell into a sea.[30]

He hallow'd the cup which now we receive,
The pledge of our hope with Jesus to live,
(Where sorrow and sadness shall never be found)
With glory and gladness eternally crown'd.[31]

The Lord's Supper provides a real and present taste of the coming future hope and glory. With sanctifying grace, the Lord's Supper serves both as a "pledge and assurance that

---

27. Anderson, *Worship and Christian Identity*, 177. Anderson quotes Henry H. Knight, III, *The Presence of God in the Christian Life: John Wesley and the Means of Grace* (Metuchen, N.J.: Scarecrow Press, 1992), 71.

28. Daniel Brevint, *The Christian Sacrament and Sacrifice* in J. Ernest Rattenbury, *The Eucharistic Hymns of John and Charles Wesley: To Which Is Appended Wesley's Preface Extracted from Brevint's* Christian Sacrament and Sacrifice *Together with* Hymns on the Lord's Supper (London: Epworth, 1948), 153, §V.1.

29. Wesley and Wesley, "Hymn LIII," *Hymns on the Lord's Supper.*

30. Wesley and Wesley, "Hymn CI," *Hymns on the Lord's Supper.*

31. Wesley and Wesley, "Hymn XCV," *Hymns on the Lord's Supper.*

God will, as it were, keep *his* side of the covenantal agreement."[32] The Lord's Supper is a chief means of this weekly growth and healing.

Danger of a Static View of Sanctification

Unfortunately, some in the Wesleyan tradition have failed to appreciate the ongoing healing offered in sanctification. Wesley often speaks about entire sanctification as *being perfected in love*. Linguistically, we tend to think of perfection as a completed state without error or blemish, which has led many either to deny that entire sanctification is possible in this life, or to assume that no more healing is needed once someone is entirely sanctified. The Church of the Nazarene often uses static language to describe sanctification. Article of Faith X in the 2005 version of Nazarene doctrine stated:

> We believe that entire sanctification is that act of God, subsequent to regeneration, by which believers are made free from original sin, or depravity, and brought into a state of entire devotement to God, and the holy obedience of love made perfect. It is wrought by the baptism of the Holy Spirit, and comprehends in one experience the cleansing of the heart from sin. . . . Entire Sanctification is provided by the blood of Jesus, is wrought instantaneously by faith, preceded by faith, preceded by entire consecration; and to this work and state of grace the Holy Spirit bears witness.[33]

This "instantaneous" state of entire sanctification is often misunderstood as sinless perfection. The word "perfect" begs for hermeneutical work by contemporary

---

32. Borgen, *John Wesley on the Sacraments*, 80.

33. Church of the Nazarene, "Articles of Faith: X. Christian Holiness and Entire Sanctification," Church Constitution, *Manual: 2005–2009* (Kansas City, MO: Nazarene Publishing House, 2005), 34–35. It is worth mentioning that revisions to this Article of Faith since have worked to celebrate both the power of the instantaneous work of God and also dynamic growth and maturing in Christ.

Wesley scholars. The term "perfection" in theology is often assumed to come from the Latin term *perfectum*, which assumes a finished and complete work. But Wesley's doctrine of perfection is more faithfully seen as descended from the Latin *perfectio*—the ongoing process of being perfected, the process of being healed to love.[34] If God granted us a static *perfectum*, we would no longer need to confess our sins, would no longer need God's continual healing. Here again the *ordo salutis* sets up a tension between justification and sanctification. Juridically, one can claim justification, pardon, and forgiveness as a state with respect to the debt being paid. As relational healing, in contrast, sanctification is a renewal in the image of God, healing the disease of self-inwardness, and must eschew any terminology that implies completion. Therefore, while sanctification continually heals and anticipates its full consummation, God's present healing leads to joy and thanksgiving. Yet this growth in healing—this pledge of the present and coming renewal—is not an isolated or monadic pilgrimage.

#3: United to Be the Body of Christ

Just as baptism is one's initiation into the church, renewal in the image of God—the gift of sanctification—also has an ecclesial dimension. The gift of sanctifying grace offered in the Lord's Supper unifies and renews the church. To be created in the *imago Dei* is a communal theological anthropology. Being healed to love God more fully simultaneously moves one to loving self and others more fully. John 17 plays an important role in Wesley's understanding of perfection in ecclesial unity. As God sanctifies Christians, God simultaneously joins and unifies the church through its healing. *Hymns on the Lord's Supper* offers a celebration of this perfection moving into ecclesial unity:

---

34. Khoo, *Wesleyan Eucharistic Spirituality*, 176.

We now forgiveness have,
We feel his work begun,
And he shall fully save,
And perfect us in one,
Shall soon in all his image dressed
Receive us to the marriage-feast.[35]

The sense of being perfected in one is present in several Wesley hymns, all connected to John 17.[36] "Hymn #426" speaks about how this redemption perfects in one.

The cov'nant of redemption seal,
The depth of love, of God, reveal,
And speak us perfected in one.[37]

The editors of the *Bicentennial Edition* of Wesley's *Works* suggest that Wesley likely had in mind John 17:23 when writing this stanza: "I in them and you in me, that they may become completely one, so that the world may know that you have sent me and have loved them even as you have loved me" (NRSVUE). Wesley envisions a communal perfection in one being offered by God, not a solitary achievement of piety. Therefore, any sense of individual perfection misses the mark.

The Lord's Supper is a primary occasion where God offers sanctifying grace, healing persons to love God and others in unity in the church. Wesley believed deeply that God makes the church one in the celebration of the Eucharist: "For it is this communion which makes us all one. We being many are yet, as it were, but different parts of one and the same broken bread, which we receive to unite us in

---

35. Wesley and Wesley, "Hymn CXI," *Hymns on the Lord's Supper.*

36. See Wesley, *A Collection of Hymns for the Use of the People Called Methodists,* #294, #373, #491; and "Appendix C, #317 (*Works of John Wesley,* 7:448, 545, 680, 732).

37. Wesley, *A Collection of Hymns,* #426, *Works of John Wesley,* 7:603.

one body."[38] The Lord's Supper and the sanctifying gift offered must never be seen as individualized growth toward a higher rung of pious spirituality. "Hymn CLXV" in *Hymns on the Lord's Supper* affirms the Eucharist as the occasion of this unity:

> How happy are thy servants, Lord,
> Who thus remember thee!
> What tongue can tell our sweet accord,
> Our perfect harmony!
>
> Who thy mysterious Supper share,
> Here at thy Table fed,
> Many, and yet but one we are,
> One undivided bread.
>
> One with the Living Bread Divine,
> Which now by faith we eat,
> Our hearts, and minds, and spirits join,
> And all in Jesus meet.
>
> So dear the tie where souls agree
> In Jesu's dying love;
> Then only can it closer be,
> When all are join'd above.[39]

Here, Charles and John speak from the center of the greater Christian eucharistic tradition that affirms that a primary gift of the Eucharist is joining believers together into the body of Christ. Although the Wesleys would not have had access to the *Didache*, an early teaching document for the Christian church, several themes offer a striking similarity. The Wesleys in "Hymn CLXV" talk about the church as "one

---

38. Wesley, "Notes on St Paul's First Epistle to the Corinthians," *Explanatory Notes upon the New Testament* (London: Bowyer, 1755), http://wesley.nnu.edu /john-wesley/john-wesleys-notes-on-the-bible/notes-on-st-pauls-first-epistle-to -the-corinthians/#Chapter+X. See also Wesley's note on John 17:23 in the same resource.

39. Wesley and Wesley, "Hymn CLXV," *Hymns on the Lord's Supper.*

undivided bread." The *Didache* prays: "As this broken bread was scattered over the mountains, and when brought together became one, so let your church be brought together from the ends of the earth into your kingdom."[40]

An individualistic spirituality cannot renew persons in the image of God. Love moves one *for, to,* and *with* all others. Love unites. In contrast, separation within the body is, according to Wesley, a sin and a failure to love:

> It is evil in itself. To separate ourselves from a body of living Christians with whom we were before united is a grievous breach of the law of love. It is the nature of love to unite us together, and the greater the love the stricter the union. And while this continues in its strength nothing can divide those whom love has united. It is only when our love grows cold that we can think of separating from our brethren. And this is certainly the case with any who willingly separate from their Christian brethren. The pretenses for separation may be innumerable, but want of love is always the real cause; otherwise they would still hold the unity of the spirit in the bond of peace.[41]

God's filling the believer with love fosters a close communion among believers and with God. In this communion, God renews the church into one as the body of Christ. This renewing in love occurs ecclesially and sacramentally both in the sacraments of baptism and in the Lord's Supper; both serve as divine events renewing our unity *in* and *as* the body of Christ, crucified and resurrected.

Borgen recognizes this perfection in unity as part of Wesley's understanding of sanctification. Borgen concludes that the doctrine of perfection and sanctification is a "union

---

40. *Didache,* in R. C. D. Jasper and G. J. Cuming, ed., *Prayers of the Eucharist, Early and Reformed: Texts Translated and Edited with Introductions* (Collegeville, MN: Liturgical Press, 1990), 23.

41. Wesley, "Sermon 75: On Schism," *Works of John Wesley,* 3:64, §1.11.

and communion of all true believers. It is a union of love, holiness and perfection, expressed especially in the somewhat cryptic phrase, 'be perfected (sanctified) in One.'"[42] This communal growth in love, being renewed in the image of God, seeks to unite and renew the church. "When we are born again, then our sanctification, our inward and outward holiness begins, and thenceforward we are gradually to 'grow up into him who is our Head.'"[43] God sanctifies us and renews us into God's image as the body of Christ.

With the celebration of the present unity fashioned at the Table, the eschatological tension reminds the church of the disunity that marks the present fractured Table. Therefore, the Table celebrates both what *is* and what *will be,* which simultaneously illuminates what is currently not. The ecclesial renewal at the Table forms the very center of the church as the body of the crucified and resurrected Christ.

---

42. Borgen, *John Wesley on the Sacraments,* 216.

43. Wesley, "Sermon 45: The New Birth," *Works of John Wesley,* 2:198, §IV.3. Cf. Ephesians 4:15.

The Sacraments in Communal Worship

Now that we have considered the Wesleyan celebration of salvation and specifically the gifts of preventing, justifying, and sanctifying grace, the focus moves to how communal worship participates in the ongoing healing God is working in the world. This section will consider briefly communal worship more broadly, then in turn examine the sacraments of baptism and the Lord's Supper more specifically.

What does it mean that the church is a body? Bodies work. Bodies *do* stuff. Bodies act. Bodies are acted upon. The volume in this series on *The Church* celebrates how the church is and more fully becomes the body of the crucified and resurrected Christ. What specifically is this body invited to be and do? Jesus Christ, within the triune God, is the central foundation upon which this body of Christ lives and moves and has its being—all through the power of the Holy Spirit, the wind and breath of God. All bodies breathe. Inhale. Exhale. God breathes in persons in communal worship to then be breathed out in doxological mission. In my book *Created to Worship*, I offer this theology of communal worship:

> Christian communal worship is the glorification of God and the sanctifi-

cation of humanity as a divine-human event where God offers transformation and healing to help people become more fully what God created them to be and do. God breathes (inhales) and gathers in individual Christians to heal, transform, and renew them as the body of Christ to breathe (exhale) them out to continue the ministry of the incarnation that participates in the kingdom of God more fully coming. The consummation of the kingdom will come and God will be all in all.[1]

For this conversation it seems crucial to proclaim that communal worship is *the very purpose of the church's existence*. To say it another way, the church's ability to exist and its reason *for* existence is communal worship. Through communal worship the triune God continues to heal, redeem, restore, renew, and form the church as the body of the crucified and resurrected Christ. Communal worship is primary. It is central to celebrate that, just like each human being's daily existence is gifted from the very breath of God, similarly the body of Christ also can only exist by the power of such breath—the Spirit of God. The

---

1. Brent D. Peterson, *Created to Worship: God's Invitation to Become Fully Human* (Kansas City, MO: Beacon Hill Press of Kansas City, 2012), 11.

liturgical rhythm of communal worship gives the church its breath from God.

Hebrews 10:25 encourages us to keep being gathered for encouragement and edification. What should this body do in communal worship? The young Pentecost church in Acts 2 affirms that "the believers devoted themselves to the apostles' teaching, to the community, to their shared meals, and to their prayers" (v. 42). John Wesley celebrates these central practices by drawing upon the Anglican Articles of Faith: "A true church is a congregation of faithful people wherein the true Word of God is preached and the sacraments duly administered."[2]

Section 1 was essential to name the foundation of a Wesleyan soteriology and theology of communal worship. A discussion of the sacraments without these theological imaginations and liturgical practices would miss the fullest celebration of the sacraments. In section 2, we will consider a broader understanding of sacramentality in the Wesleyan tradition and look specifically at the sacraments of baptism and the Lord's Supper. Each consideration will begin with a look at the primary theology of that sacrament followed by a chapter describing best practices.

---

2. Wesley, "February 6, 1740," *Works of John Wesley: Journal and Diaries II*, 19:138.

SIX

Sacraments: Initiation and Sustenance of the Martyr Church

Within the Wesleyan tradition, the centrality of the sacraments cannot be overstated. We have already discussed how John and Charles largely adopted and celebrated the sacramental theology that was handed down to them by the Church of England in the eighteenth century, yet their intensity and devotion to the sacraments were novel, forever grounding the renewal movement God began through them. This chapter will explore a broad view of sacraments in the Wesleyan tradition, first considering what a sacrament *is*, then celebrating the context of a sacramental world, the gift of remembrance, the union of Word and sacrament, the essence of responsible grace, and the union of personal and ecclesial healing through the sacraments.

What Is a Sacrament?

The term "sacrament" derives etymologically from the notion of *mystery*, and celebrating the sacraments *as* a mystery is a tremendous gift for the church. Just as the church attempts to reflect on the great mystery of the triune God, so too the church leans into the mystery of the sacraments with humble joy. The context of glorious mystery always reminds the church that, as it writes and reflects on these tremendous gifts, the discourse should always be done in a spirit of praise and doxology rather than under the premise of cognitive mastery. In addition, even as we have celebrated God's unique and powerful presence in the sacraments, we also affirm that God is not *exhaustively* present. Awareness of God's absence creates space for an encounter with the mysterious, self-giving presence of God.

For the Wesleys, the sacraments are a *means of grace*—a mediation of God's undeserved, healing, transforming presence. As such, the sacraments are events of God's self-giving. This self-giving is connected to the very center of God's *kenotic* nature. The *kenosis* of God is most keenly celebrated in the Christ hymn in Philippians 2: "Though he was in the form of God, he did not consider being equal with God something to exploit. But he emptied himself by taking the form of a slave and by becoming like human beings" (vv. 6–7). This emptying did not mean God ceased to be divine; instead, it was a revelation that the nature of the triune God is pouring out (*kenosis*) in love for the life, redemption, and flourishing of all creation. The sacraments are a further embodiment of this divine self-giving, *kenotic* love.

The sacraments are "the love of God made visible."[1] The love is God's continual self-giving to creation.[2] When Christians testify that all things are created and sustained by God's presence, we affirm that nothing exists apart from God's continuing life-giving of God's self. In this way all of creation is sacramental. All things that exist are good, true, and beautiful expressions of God's *kenotic* self-giving. This is not to say all things are God (pantheism). Pantheism fails to affirm God's transcendence (otherness) and to distinguish Creator from creation. Celebrating a sacramental

---

1. James F. White, *The Sacraments in Protestant Practice and Faith* (Nashville: Abingdon, 1999), 13.

2. The term "self-giving" in connection to God can be seen as problematic. First, what does it mean for God to *have* a self? Moreover, God as triune must inform this notion of giving and receiving love in the divine perichoretic dance. This is why the idea of God's self-giving is really an analogy of naming God's triune economic love poured out upon creation. The incarnation is precisely an act of triune, self-giving, *kenotic* love.

Wesleyan Sacramental Theology

Protestants only affirm two sacraments, whereas our Roman Catholic and Orthodox Christian siblings observe seven: baptism, confirmation, Eucharist, reconciliation, anointing the sick, marriage, and ordination of clergy. Though Protestants certainly affirm all seven practices as important and holy, we elevate only baptism and Eucharist to the level of sacrament because those are the two that are commanded by Christ in the New Testament.

world names God as the source and sustainer of all. Genesis 1 asserts that all creation is good, but sin is a disease that God is working to heal by inviting and empowering creatures to participate in the ongoing healing from sin to love.

James White notes that self-giving is inherent among the human existence. Infants cannot exist apart from the time, energy, resources, and sustenance provided by parents and caregivers. "Each meal we feed a small child is more than food—it is a self-giving mediated through feeding."[3] Yet the human experience is not simply about an economic exchange of goods and resources to survive but a personal web of relationships. White compares the self-giving of humanity to illuminate God's self-giving, which is the ground of all self-giving. White notes that self-giving is expressing love as "the unselfish pouring out of self for the benefit of another, without thought of return."[4] As a loving mother nurses her infant, there is no expectation for the child to return a *quid pro quo*. The love of the mother is intended for self-giving. While human self-giving may be quantified as milk, time, or borrowing a truck, this giving at its best is about a giving and sharing of self. These things are offered as relational gifts of love.

White notes the transition when thinking about God's self-giving named in communal worship that empowers humans in thanksgiving to offer ourselves back to God. This offering and receiving are at the heart of the sacraments: "Public worship depends constantly on the use of actions as means of expressing God's self-giving to us and our self-giving to God and to one another."[5] This does not mean humans and God are equal partners with equal powers and equal self-giving. It is God's good design to invite

---

3. James F. White, *Sacraments as God's Self Giving* (Nashville: Abingdon, 2001), 14.

4. White, *Sacraments as God's Self Giving*, 15.

5. White, *Sacraments as God's Self Giving*, 22.

humans to participate in the ongoing healing of creation, specifically around the sacraments. Humans participate in the self-giving of God in many other places—but especially the sacraments. White notes that the sacraments serve as unique activity in communal worship: "People perform [the sacraments], but through them experience God's self-giving."[6]

Every time I am asked to anoint and pray over someone, we are responding to Scripture's invitation to ask and request prayer for wisdom and healing for illness (see James 5:14). Yet I am not the source of the wisdom, comfort, and healing. God is the source of power that ministers are invited to draw upon in God's self-giving. In the sacraments of baptism and the Lord's Supper, the minister is a vehicle for mediating God's self-giving. Martin Luther notes, "For man baptizes, and yet does not baptize. He baptizes in that he performs the work of immersing the person to be baptized, but he does not baptize, because in so doing he acts not on his own authority but in God's stead."[7] Humans are performing the actions of immersion, of breaking the bread, and of passing the cup, and in this way are giving of their human ministry. "Human beings perform the outward action, the visible sacrament; but it is God who acts in self-giving to give the inward fruit that makes it a sacrament and not just another sign-act."[8]

The emphasis is on human action that God has ordained, empowered, and equipped and then sacrificially gives as the visible, transforming encounter of love. White suggests that God can, could, and sometimes does bypass human cooperation and visible signs. Yet White contends that God recognized "our human actions are needed to give

---

6. White, *Sacraments as God's Self Giving*, 22–23.

7. Martin Luther, "Babylonian Captivity of the Church," *Luther's Works* XXXVI (Philadelphia: Fortress Press, 1959), 62.

8. White, *Sacraments as God's Self Giving*, 23.

visible form, to make incarnate the divine action. Because our humanity needs actions as outward and visible signs of self-giving, God gives us sacraments so that we can know that which is inward and spiritual."[9] From pedagogical strategy to cognitive science, to sociological observation of human behavior and ritual, the more senses involved and the more visible the action, the more it impacts and transforms the humans engaged and involved.

A Wesleyan theological anthropology (why we believe God created humanity) contends that humans are deeply experiential as well as relational. Therefore, God's desire and invitation for humans to participate in God's self-giving is intentional. While humans do not save or heal, God's desire to allow humans to participate in the healing of other humans is a tremendous and transforming gift in the church. Bonds are forged as humans are invited to participate in the transformational work God is doing in creation.

Holy Spirit as God's Healing in the Sacraments

The sacramental matter itself (water, bread, and wine or juice) is not what heals and saves. The Spirit working *through* these common elements transforms them—and us—in the sacramental encounter of transformation. The Wesleys clearly affirmed the dynamic power of the Spirit in the sacraments. For John Wesley, none of the means of grace have any healing power apart from the Holy Spirit:

> We allow likewise that all outward means whatever, if separate from the Spirit of God, cannot profit at all, cannot conduce in any degree either to the knowledge or love of God. Without controversy, the help that is done upon earth, he doth it himself. It is he alone who, by his own almighty power, worketh in us what

---

9. White, *Sacraments as God's Self Giving*, 24.

is pleasing in his sight. And all outward things, unless he work in them and by them, are mere weak and beggarly elements.[10]

The Holy Spirit is the power of God in all the sacraments. Christ's presence heals and transforms through the sacraments by the power of the Holy Spirit.

Sacraments in the Wesleyan Tradition

Three ideas will briefly explore the sacraments in the Wesleyan tradition.

First, the sacraments not only celebrate what God has done in the past but also affirm God's dynamic presence now, offering healing and transforming, which is also grounded in the eschatological hope of what is to come in the future.

Second, Wesleyans celebrate God's desire to heal and transform while inviting and empowering persons to respond and live into God's invitations to heal.

Third, the healing and transformation of the sacraments is both personal and communal, and a participation in the further inbreaking of the kingdom of God.

#1: Remember the Past, Celebrate Present Healing, Live into Future Hope

The sacraments celebrate what God has been doing since the dawn of creation. A central piece of liturgies of both baptism and the Lord's Supper is something we often call "memorialism," remembering how God has been faithful in the past. The Jewish worship calendar—from Rosh Hashanah to Passover to Shavout—is rife with annual festivals that celebrate and remember God's past faithfulness. One of the key sins attributed to God's people in Scripture

---

10. Wesley, "Sermon 16: The Means of Grace," *Works of John Wesley,* 1:382, §II.3.

is a failure to remember God. Failure to remember God's past acts often leads to present lives that do not embrace the hope and promise of being covenant people. Sacraments remember God's saving activity in the past.

Yet sacramental memory is much more than a sentimental, nostalgic look backward. Grace in the sacraments is best celebrated as the undeserved healing and transforming presence of God's *kenotic*, self-giving love. God is present in the sacraments offering healing and transformation *now*. The idea of *anamensis* (a Greek word that is often translated as "remember") is not simply about looking back but also celebrating a present encounter with God. In both the Lord's Supper and baptism, God offers and invites persons into a healing from sin to love. A failure to participate in the sacraments is missing out on the present encounter of healing God offers.

#2: Word and Sacrament: United in Continual Divine Self-Giving

As sacraments, baptism and the Lord's Supper are always connected to proclamation of and encounter with the Word. The term "word" has a variety of meanings in Scripture. In the creation story in Genesis 1, the Word spoken by God creates. In the beginning of the Gospel of John, the Son is referred to as the *logos* (translated as "Word") who became incarnate in the person of Jesus Christ. The term "word of God" is also connected to the reading and preaching of Scripture in public worship (see Hebrews 4:12). The proclamation of Scripture is empowered by the Spirit for a dynamic encounter in the church: "Through the working of the Spirit, the past historical work of Christ and the eternal reality of Christ are both given to us in worship as a present event."[11] White rightly notes that the proclama-

____

11. White, *Sacraments as God's Self Giving*, 27.

tion of Scripture is not simply telling a story of the past but an invitation to a fresh, self-giving, divine encounter with Jesus Christ. "Each service of worship becomes a new creation through the proclamation of the Word as a means of Christ's self-giving afresh."[12] This dynamic presence of Christ by the Spirit is central to a Wesleyan understanding of both the sacraments of baptism and the Lord's Supper, and frames specifically the conversation about the presence of Christ in the Lord's Supper.

The church has also, at its best, included the readings and proclamation of Scripture in all celebrations of the sacraments as an encounter with the Word, who is Jesus Christ. Including Scripture in the observance of sacraments properly reflects that all sacraments are part of a celebration of Word and water and Table. Word—the reading and preaching of Scripture, empowered by the Spirit—connects and links baptism and the Lord's Supper as one event. "Word and sacrament are not distinct realities but part of the same event. It is one and the same Christ who is given to us in both preaching and action."[13] Historically the term "Eucharist" did not refer only to the bread and wine but also to the entire service of Scripture read and proclaimed, prayer sung and spoken, and the administration of the Lord's Supper.

Many liturgical traditions recite a prayer of illumination before the reading of Scripture. The United Methodist *Book of Worship* offers this example: "Lord, open our hearts and minds, by the power of the Holy Spirit, that, as the Scriptures are read and your Word proclaimed, we may hear with joy what you say to us today."[14] Notice the care of the prayer to distinguish between Scripture and Jesus as the

---

12. White, *Sacraments as God's Self Giving*, 27.

13. White, *Sacraments as God's Self Giving*, 27.

14. United Methodist Church, *United Methodist Book of Worship* (Nashville: The United Methodist Publishing House, 1992), 34.

Word. In theology and worship, precision is necessary, so guiding local congregations on the Word as Scripture and the Word as Jesus is helpful. It may be pastorally helpful to model the distinction by referring to the Bible as Scripture and Jesus as the Word of God. In this way the Scriptures, by the power of the Holy Spirit, illuminate and help make the Word of God—Jesus Christ—dynamically present in *kenotic*, self-giving ways.

Some worship traditions also invite the Spirit to empower and speak through the preacher. An example of this invitation might be: *Gracious God, send your Spirit to anoint the lips of our minister of the Word, Olivia. May she be empowered to faithfully proclaim the good news of Jesus Christ as the Scriptures are broken open.* This prayer empowering the minister alludes to another connection between the service of the Word (Scripture proclaimed and preached) and the Lord's Supper. Just as the self-giving of the triune God continues at each celebration of the Eucharist as the body of Christ is broken and his blood poured out, so too in the service of the Word does Christ's self-giving continue as, through Scripture, the Word is read (broken open) and poured out (preached). Empowered by the Spirit, the reading of Scripture, the prophetic proclamation in preaching, and the celebration of the sacraments all point to and become an occasion for the continual self-giving of Christ.

The sacraments celebrate what God has done in the past (memorialism) as well as what God is doing now (means of grace), and all of it is grounded in the promise for what God will do in the future (eschatological hope). The sacraments participate in the further inbreaking of the kingdom of God, thus providing a foundation of hope that often invades an uncertain present. The hope of the kingdom of God that is already here and also yet to come affirms that each celebration of the sacraments is another movement into and toward the promised and coming kingdom.

#3: Personal and Ecclesial: Never Private or Individualistic

One of the dangers for Christians in the United States (and perhaps other parts of the globe) is the emphasis on having a personal relationship with Jesus. Although it is essential that each person respond as much as they are able, the Christian life is not an individual quest for personal piety. The full celebration of being Christian is in being part of the church—past, present, and future. Individuals respond to God's invitation to healing, forgiveness, and life, yet that healing *includes* incorporation into the church as the body of Christ. In the sacraments, we can experience healing and salvation that are deeply connected to our identity in the body of Christ. There is no such thing as an individual Christian—Christians are *always* part of the body of the crucified and resurrected Christ. This body includes the value of each person but also recognizes that the full hope of healing is in our presence in the covenant body of Christ, the church.

Similarly, the sacraments are never to be performed privately for only a select few. Throughout church history, the very rich have often sought home or private baptisms because they only wanted a few select (that is, elite) members of the church present. The universal church condemns such practice. A basic and necessary facet of what makes a gathering a Christian worship service is the public invitation to all. All who desire to come are welcome.[15] When we talk about condemning sacraments celebrated in private, we are talking about privacy of convenience, not privacy of necessity. There are times when people cannot make it to public gatherings because they are incarcerated, hospitalized, homebound, or experiencing other extenuating

---

15. Certainly, in some world areas where having a Christian worship service is illegal, care must be taken.

circumstances. In these cases, the local church has a duty and obligation to go to prisons, hospitals, and homes in joyful hospitality in order to renew the covenantal relationship and include these members of the body of Christ in the communal worship ministry.

Responding to God's Grace

One of the most important Wesleyan theological texts from the end of the twentieth century is Randy Maddox's *Responsible Grace*. Maddox combines historical and theological perspectives from both Wesley brothers and the larger Wesleyan tradition. The title provides a window into the center of the Wesleyan theological universe. As opposed to other faith traditions that emphasize God's sovereignty of power and grace that cannot be thwarted or opposed, the Wesleyan tradition affirms a sovereignty of love. Although some theological traditions claim that God's grace, once extended, cannot be rejected, Wesleyans celebrate a God who does not overpower or control us but who seeks, woos, and invites us, giving us the option to accept or reject God's invitation.

This idea of response is essential in the sacraments as well. Although God is the primary and initiatory actor, the healing presence of God offered in the sacraments requires a response. Contrary to the idea that our response, or even our ability to respond, is any type of achievement of our own, the Wesleyan tradition affirms that God is the only one who makes a response possible—even if that response is rejection. This divine-human cooperation—where God invites us to be healed and transformed into love and then empowers us to respond—grounds the Wesleyan understanding of salvation.

In the sacraments of baptism and the Lord's Supper, as God is present and invites the church into deeper healings of love, humans—by the power of the Spirit—are invited to

Wesleyan Sacramental Theology

In the sacramental practices of baptism and the Lord's Supper, God acts as a fulfillment of God's promise and command offered in Scripture. The sacraments are also evangelistic, affirming that, in order for the full flourishing of the healing God desires to do, we must continually respond to God's invitations to healing and transformation into a vibrant faith of holy love.

continually respond to this invitation to heal in order that love might flourish.

Faithful to Tradition

Throughout Christian history the church has passed down some essential elements to the liturgical practices of baptism and the Lord's Supper. While there are some important distinctions in practice within the broader Christian family, there are a few aspects that are required in order to be recognized as Christian sacraments.

In my classroom, I like to hold up a green marker and ask my students what color it is. Most of the time they all say green. I then remind them that it could also be called *verde* or *verte* or other words for green in other languages. I then ask if we could start calling that same color "yellow" instead. With prodding, I convince them that there is nothing scientific about what they see that prevents us from renaming the color that our culture has decided to call green. The terms "green" and "yellow" are simply words that serve as symbolic metaphors that we have agreed to for clarity in communication. I tell them we can start the green-to-yellow revolution. We could start a broad social media campaign and see how fast we kick off a viral trend. Then I have them imagine they are successful in their efforts, and what we used to call green, we now call yellow. I then ask, "What problems would emerge from such a project?" One of the problems would be how to chart history. Our new yellow would be disconnected from the past.

Tradition is important when it comes to the sacraments of baptism and Lord's Supper. Tradition is not a legalistic taskmaster but a provider of a rich narrative that also invites a conversation to hear, listen, and grapple. Any tradition that disallows questions is a tradition that is both weak and insecure. It is important to note that some aspects of sacramental practice have evolved with thoughtful listening, reflection, and conversation. Some of these transitions have resulted in unique practices among the broader Christian family. Yet there is a core of faithful continuity that has remained. I encourage my students to, first, drink deeply of the church's liturgical practices and attempt to understand the narrative that grounds the church's sacramental practices. Then, only with a deep listening and extended broad conversation across the universal church, some adjustments and tweaks may be considered.

The sacraments are not our playthings. While God inspires ongoing contextual creativity, care must be taken to honor the deep tradition of the church. Pastors who have failed to drink deeply of the church's sacramental tradition often end up engaging in practices that are less than faithful. It is not that these pastors *seek* to do harm, but they exhibit a failure to be immersed in the church's deep tradition. Naïve creativity may move sacramental practice outside of what is recognizable to the broader church and lead to malformation or distortion. Without care, our sacramental practice can turn from what the church calls green to what we call yellow, so that the larger church cannot recognize it.

There has been diversity and creativity in the church's sacramental practices, past and present, especially early in the church's history. However, over the past 1,500 years, those practices have found greater familiarity and continuity. We do not blindly do what the church has always done just for the sake of it, but deep immersion in tradition and practice can allow faithful creativity in fresh expressions to flourish.

SEVEN

The Sacrament of Baptism

The power, terror, and chaos of water are seen throughout Scripture. In Genesis 1, God's exhale pushes the waters back to allow the land to emerge. In the story of Noah, God's inhale allows the seas to overtake all land—an undoing of creation. Baby Moses is set adrift upon the waters in order to be protected. Then God uses the staff of Moses to separate the waters of the Red Sea to allow the people of Israel to pass on dry ground before unleashing those same waters to drown Pharaoh's horses and chariots in the depths of the sea. Joshua leads God's people across the Jordan River by the presence of the Ark of the Covenant. Then later, in the waters of that same river, the prophet John the Baptist invites God's people not to a kingdom of land and power but to repentance and greater faithfulness.

Water takes life; it also cleanses and gives life. Water is powerful. Even decades into the twenty-first century, with all our technological advancements, we can still stand at the rim of the Grand Canyon in Arizona or on a ledge near Niagara Falls or on a boat in the middle of the Pacific Ocean and find ourselves in awe of this mysterious force that can be harnessed, redirected, and used for our good—yet cannot be fully contained. One tsunami can devastate entire towns and villages, yet water is also the source of life. Humans can survive without food for up to three weeks, but without water we can only live for three days. Those who have lived in the parts of the world where the sun scorches the desert can especially attest to water's ability to quench thirst and bring life.

It is the Christian conviction that the Lord of the waters has ordained the sacrament of baptism to be a means of drowning, cleansing, and birthing of new life of water and Spirit. A Wesleyan theology of baptism embodies the central paradoxical tensions of Wesley and his ecclesial and theological heirs. Wesley's writings on baptism also testify to his own growth and maturation. The evolution of Wesley's vibrant sacramental piety not only shaped his teaching and preaching of baptism but also influenced his more mature soteriology. God is the primary actor who graciously acts preveniently to pardon and cleanse our sin and inherited guilt through the gracious work of the triune God. The gift of Christ, by the Spirit, at the will of the Father is the *sacrament* of God to the church. Yet these gifts of God must be *responded to* for the full healing of God's gracious presence to transform into maturity in holiness. This pious response is not a work or merit but an act of worship—a doxology. This passion of a sacramental piety guides a baptismal mosaic of praise.

The theological conversation of the great gift and mystery of baptism begins through immersion into the immediate days before Christian baptism emerged, then reflects on how baptism is a drowning and cleansing in the process of the salvation story, a fellowship in Christ's death and resurrection, a covenant initiation into the church, one's initial justification, new birth, and adoption. Along the way the conversation will work to faithfully track John Wesley's journey and passions surrounding baptism to provide the Wesleyan tradition a fuller celebration and practice of the gift of baptism. For some this chapter may become too technical and tedious. Since the medium and matter of theology lives in iconic words, precision and care are required

Wesleyan Sacramental Theology

The sacrament of baptism is a triune act of joining and fellowship in Christ's death and resurrection as a covenantal initiation into the church. This means of grace offers both the justifying grace of forgiveness and the healing of the new birth as we are indelibly marked by the Spirit as God's beloved children, set forth to live into further healing in Christlikeness.

to more faithfully live in awe of the mystery God is working in the world.

Johannine Baptisms

John the Baptist was a prophet calling people into the physical wilderness to repent and turn back from the metaphorical wilderness of their sin (see Mark 4:1–8). Prevailing Jewish custom around baptism was that it was used as a means of inducting gentile converts into the Jewish faith. John's baptism uniquely called those already in the Jewish faith to repent of their sins, seeking God's forgiveness and transformation. Jesus found John's ministry to be authentic and true, and he presented himself to John for baptism (see Matthew 4:3:13–17; Mark 1:9–11; Luke 3:21–22; John 1:29–34).

Jesus's baptism appears scandalous at first glance. Baptism was for sinners. Was Jesus a sinner? Absolutely not! (see Hebrews 4:15). Yet, as the Messiah of the Jews, and of all humanity, Jesus submitted to baptism as a representative model for all humanity in need of God's cleansing and also as his personal act of humility and devotion toward God. Jesus's baptism was a willing surrender, a yielding of his life back to God as an act of thanksgiving and devotion. It is right to affirm that Jesus did not need cleansing of his own personal sin, but his act of obedience and submission to God through John's baptism was a powerful declaration recorded in Scripture of the *kenotic* offering of his life to God as modeled to him by his mother, Mary. The Gospel accounts of the baptism also relay divine words from heaven expressing love, joy, and pleasure in Jesus. His baptism by John inaugurates Jesus's ministry as he is led by the Spirit into the wilderness to encounter temptation.

The inclusion of Jesus's baptism in all four Gospels resulted in the church's emphasis on the importance of this sacramental act of humble devotion by Jesus followed by a response of love and commission from God. Yet Jesus himself did not receive a *Christian* baptism. Baptism that is specifically Christian symbolizes our death to sin, our rising with Christ in resurrection, and our entrance and participation into Jesus's body—the church. Rob Staples notes that Jesus's disciples did baptize during Jesus's ministry as a continuation of John's baptism ministry of repentance. Yet even this practice was not *Christian* baptism (see John 4:2). John the Baptist himself announces the unique gifts of Christian baptism: "I baptize with water those of you who have changed your hearts and lives. The one who is coming after me is stronger than I am. I'm not worthy to carry his sandals. He will baptize you with the Holy Spirit and with fire" (Matthew 3:11). Baptism by the Spirit and fire points to the way Christian baptism "had its real beginning at Pentecost."[1]

Becoming part of Jesus's body and blood begins at baptism. The church was commissioned by Christ as the Spirit blew the church to all the corners of the earth. In our going, Christians are to make disciples of all nations, living into the calling given to Abraham, baptizing in the name of the Father, Son, and the Holy Spirit (see Matthew 28:19). The early church recognized that baptism was both a gift and a command. Concluding his sermon on the day of Pentecost, Peter declared, "Change your hearts and lives. Each of you must be baptized in the name of Jesus Christ for the forgiveness of your sins. Then you will receive the gift of the Holy Spirit" (Acts 2:38).

---

1. Rob L. Staples, *Outward Sign and Inward Grace: The Place of Sacraments in Wesleyan Spirituality* (Kansas City, MO: Beacon Hill Press of Kansas City, 1991), 121.

Drowning and Cleansing,
Death and Resurrection

Baptism is a covenantal joining into Christ's life and ministry. By the will of the Father, empowered by the Spirit, the Son of God became incarnate in the person of Jesus Christ. Jesus serves as the Savior of and High Priest over all creation. Believers, as part of the church, are united with Christ in his death and resurrection. Although the early church's metaphors and symbols for Christian baptism varied, one theme that arose was connected to a dynamic Pauline text:

> Therefore, we were buried together with him through baptism into his death, so that just as Christ was raised from the dead through the glory of the Father, we too can walk in newness of life. If we were united together in a death like his, we will also be united together in a resurrection like his. This is what we know: the person that we used to be was crucified with him in order to get rid of the corpse that had been controlled by sin. That way we wouldn't be slaves to sin anymore, because a person who has died has been freed from sin's power.
> (Romans 6:4–7)

Following the example of this scripture, the church began to affirm that Christians are united in Christ's death and resurrection in the waters of baptism. The gift of baptism is a drowning of pain, sin, and death. It is also a resurrection of healing in love for abundant life as believers fellowship and join in Christ's death and resurrection.

Just as the Israelites, upon entering the Red Sea, were invited to die to their identity as slaves, and exit the Red Sea as the rescued and redeemed people of God, so too are Christians invited to the same. As we submit to the baptismal waters, God helps put to death the sin, pain, and despair of all we have endured and absorbed in our bodies.

This drowning is a joining in Christ's death, which was the ultimate defeat of sin and death. Without this drowning to sin, we cannot join in Christ's resurrection of new life as part of the new creation kingdom that is present and still coming. Baptism is a drowning and cleansing from sin and a new birth into resurrection life, set free from the fear of sin and death.

Baptism is a covenantal initiation into the martyr church of the life, death, resurrection, and ascension of Jesus Christ. A martyr ecclesiology is not about death, or seeking to die; it is about being set free from the power of sin and death to live into the resurrection life of hope and healing as we offer our lives back to God in thanksgiving. This fellowshiping, joining, and uniting in Christ's death and resurrection are the covenantal assertions that the sacrament of baptism is initiation into the church.

Initiation into the Martyr Church

While the celebration of justifying grace and the gift of the new birth are also part of the glorious mystery of baptism, it is important to name how the first triune movement of baptism is initiation into the martyr church as the body of the crucified and resurrected Christ. Part of the errant individual emphasis on baptism comes from a misapplication of the idea that every person must respond to God's wooing. Too often Christians conceive of their faith as "Jesus and me," as if the Christian journey is individual and private. Individually responding to God's wooing and entering into a personal relationship with Jesus absolutely does not mean we go on our own individual, private trek with Jesus. Christianity by its very nature cannot be anything but communal. God's desire for humanity is that each person be loved, valued, and nurtured as part of God's good creation, as testified by God's declaration that it was not good for Adam to be alone (see Genesis 2:18). The church confesses that God created humanity for relationship so that *love might flourish.*

Christian baptismal liturgies through the centuries have drawn upon the powerful story of the Israelites passing through the Red Sea from death to life as part of God's story of initiation into the covenant people. A contemporary baptismal liturgy in offering a prayer of thanksgiving over the water prays, "Eternal Father, when nothing existed but chaos, you swept across the dark waters and brought forth light. In the days of Noah you saved those on the ark through water. After the flood you set in the clouds a rainbow. When you saw your people as slaves in Egypt, you led them to freedom through the sea. Their children you brought through the Jordan to the land which you promised."[2] The powerful image of waters as chaos yet controlled by God is found throughout both Testaments.

When we discuss the importance of baptism and its initiatory gift, we are guided by Christian history and tradition. We have noted already the scriptures where both Jesus and Peter command (not suggest) that baptism is required for inclusion in the people of God. It has largely been affirmed throughout Christianity that those who are not baptized have not been initiated into the church and are therefore not fully part of the church. Moreover, only those who are part of the church are fully Christian. That does not mean, for Wesleyans, that the unbaptized are automatically doomed to hell. However, remember that our ultimate goal as Christians is not merely to gain heaven or avoid hell in the afterlife. The promise and hope of heaven continually meet us on earth every day, as Jesus instructed us to pray (see Matthew 6:10), and this coming of the kingdom of God to earth is the full goal of God's work.

---

2. United Methodist Church, "Thanksgiving over the Water," Baptismal Covenant I, *Book of Worship,* 90.

Remember that one of John and Charles Wesley's concerns was that so many people who were baptized in England were not living into a dynamic faith of holy love. The Wesleys' ministry was grounded on the pastoral passion that, just because someone is baptized and may even attend communal worship and partake of the Eucharist, that is not a guarantee that one's life is maturing in holy love.[3] As noted in several places in the Wesleyan tradition, persons are saved by grace through faith. Yet a faith that grows and matures in holy love responds to God's healing invitations and produces the fruit of holy love in a person's life. Wesleyans firmly celebrate that only the redeeming work of the triune God is necessary for salvation. Therefore, no one is excluded from heaven for not being baptized. However, baptism is a wonderful gift and promise in Christian discipleship. Those who have not been baptized miss out on part of the healing and ecclesial formation God desires to do in the life of the church. These considerations are why we say that believers who have not been baptized are not fully Christian.

In my U.S. context, Christianity has too often emphasized robust individualism over and against finding our identity in the church as the body of Christ. The primary goal of too many U.S. American Christians has been to have a personal (by which they often mean private) relationship with Jesus. This individualistic evangelistic focus exposes our "free church" tendencies. A free church imagination believes individual Christians come together to make the church, rather than seeing that the church is where Christians are made.[4] In my personal experience,

---

3. See John Wesley, "Sermon 45: The New Birth," *Works of John Wesley*, 1:402–03, §III:2.

4. To explore this topic further, specifically the idea of free church in comparison to other forms of ecclesial imagination, see Miroslav Volf, *After Our Likeness: The Church as the Image of the Trinity* (Grand Rapids: Eerdmans, 1998).

although I was raised in a tradition that emphasized individual faith, what ended up seeping into my bones was, ironically, the weekly participation in a dynamic and healthy local church. Emphasizing that God makes Christians through the church does not deny the importance of a personal response, but it celebrates again that union with persons from every nation and tribe is at the core of Christian salvation (see Revelation 7:9).

Adopted as Children of God

Connected to initiation is the celebration of our adoption at baptism. Baptism celebrates that Christian salvation is inherently both sacramental and ecclesial. It is sacramental as God offers transformation, wooing and empowering our response to such grace. It is ecclesial in that naming ourselves as Christian is claiming our initiation and adoption into the body of Christ, the martyr church.

My wife graduated with a degree in social work, and one of her early jobs was in the foster care and adoption department of a Midwestern state. She worked to help place children in the foster care system in permanent homes through adoption. As you probably already know or could guess, older children had a more difficult time being placed because they often had many more physical and emotional scars. Although her job involved a great deal of compassion and heartache, there was no greater joy than when she was able to help finalize an adoption. Although every situation is unique, it is important to acknowledge that there are still pain and loss in every adoption story.

On social media, several of my friends celebrate anniversary dates of finalized adoptions. These celebrations are powerful. Along with initiation into the church, baptism also celebrates our adoption into the family of God. The language of adoption frames our relationship with the body of Christ not simply as an association of like-minded people but as a close, *covenantal* commitment of the deepest kind. Unlike the worldly adoption of children—which is tinged with a shadow of sadness for altered, damaged, or terminated relationships—adoption into the family of God moves us from the individualism of death, sin, and despair into a new identity as children of God who are full of hope and life. Initiation and adoption into the body of Christ indicate that baptism is not restricted to a local church or specific denomination but is how we are made part of the universal body of the global church of Christ.

Our adoption into the family of God comes with unique blessings as heirs of God's kingdom. Wesley affirms,

> In consequence of our being made children of God, we are heirs of the kingdom of heaven. "If children," (as the apostle observes,) "then heirs, heirs of God, and joint-heirs with Christ." Herein we receive a title to, and an earnest of, "a kingdom which cannot be moved." Baptism doth now save us, if we live answerable thereto; if we repent, believe, and obey the gospel: Supposing this, as it admits us into the church here, so into glory hereafter.[5]

Those adopted are heirs of the kingdom! While Wesley's overall teaching and preaching celebrate the healing process of salvation, note his strong affirmation here of baptism's work to "save us now." But also see that this salvation is conditional: it is God's work that humans must respond to. Baptism saves *as* we repent, believe, and obey the gospel. The human response is not a work that *earns* salvation, but it responds co-operantly to God's offer of salvation.

Wesley is also quoting and drawing upon Romans 8:17: "But if we are children, we are also heirs. We are God's heirs and fellow heirs with Christ, if we really suffer with him so that we can also be glorified with him." Note the

____

5. Wesley, *Works of John Wesley: Treatise on Baptism*, 14:284, §II:5.

condition of being heirs: we suffer with Christ and thus glorify God. This idea is central to a Wesleyan martyr ecclesiology and sacramental theology: we join in Christ's death and resurrection; as such, we will suffer with Christ. The goal is not masochism but a life *immersed* in compassionate justice, *sprinkled* with grace, thanksgiving, and humility, and *poured out* by the Spirit as a drink offering for the life of the world (see Philippians 2:17).

Regeneration and Adoption

The healing of justification and the new birth are also deeply connected to the healing waters of baptism:

> By baptism, we who were "by nature children of wrath" are made the children of God. And this regeneration which our church in so many places ascribes to baptism is more than barely being admitted into the church, though commonly connected therewith; being "grafted into the body of Christ's church, we are made the children of God by adoption and grace." This is grounded on the plain words of our Lord: "Except a man be born again of water and of the Spirit, he cannot enter into the kingdom of God" (John 3:5). By water then, as a means, the water of baptism, we are regenerated or born again; whence it is also called by the apostle "the washing of regeneration." Our church therefore ascribes no greater virtue to baptism than Christ himself has done.[6]

We see Wesley affirming the great gift of baptism. Along with the language of being made children of God (adoption), this is also part of regeneration. Regeneration is connected to initial sanctification as ongoing healing into maturity in holy love—Christlikeness.

------

6. Wesley, *Works of John Wesley: Treatise on Baptism*, 14:283–84, §II.4.

Most often when discussing the salvation healing offered at baptism, the focus goes immediately to justification (forgiveness of sins), and on occasion a conversation is had about the initial sanctification that begins at baptism. Specifically within a Wesleyan celebration of the sacrament of baptism, we very intentionally first emphasize that union in Christ's death and resurrection is connected to initiation into the church and adoption as a child of God. This emphasis grounds the sacrament and the healing of salvation as thoroughly ecclesial (communal). Salvation in Christianity is deeply connected to covenantal participation in the church and adoption into the family of God.

The shared excerpt from Wesley's *Treatise on Baptism* rightfully wants to merge all these images and facets of baptism as part of the salvation story. The fullness of the salvation offered at baptism is a mosaic of multiple images. However, it is paramount that a Wesleyan understanding of salvation as seen through the sacrament of baptism be recognized as ecclesial. This strong communal emphasis does not mean there is *no* personal response, but it offers the proper context from transitioning from an isolated individual to a beloved child in the church as the body of Christ.

Regeneration and Justification at Baptism

With this firm ecclesial foundation of a Wesleyan soteriology, now the great mosaics of justification and new birth will be explored in the context of the sacrament of baptism. It is essential that these are not seen as separate from the other mosaics of dying and rising with Christ, initiation, and adoption in the church.

John Wesley does emphasize that, while God acts in the sacrament, the full adoption, covenantal membership in the church, forgiveness, and cleansing and healing from sin must be continually responded to for the full vibrancy of the sacraments to flourish. This perspective leans into the central foundation for a Wesleyan sacramental theology of a strong emphasis of God's action and human response to God's transforming power. My colleague Dean Blevins, emphasizing the importance of catechesis, has also named correctly that, while Wesley's strong encouragement for baptism never wavered, baptism must be seen not as an end but as a beginning:

> Wesley's continued fear rests with one assuming the Christian life was complete, a "landing zone" that represented a state of nominal Christian salvation. Such a view proved particularly problematic if one might "fall" into practices that "sinned away" the grace represented in baptism. More proactively, Wesley viewed the beginning of the Christian life more like a "launching pad;" the new birth ushered believers into holiness as both impetus and goal.[7]

Baptism is part of a crucial discipleship beginning in one's ongoing healing into a vibrant and maturing faith of holy love.

In chapters 4 and 5 we discussed the distinctions between justifying and sanctifying grace (that includes new birth and regeneration). In summary, justification celebrates our sins being forgiven and God declaring us righteous in the juridical (legal) pardoning from the debt and penalty of sin. Regeneration and the new birth are part of God's sanctifying grace that seeks to make us righteous as part of an ongoing cleansing. For the Wesleyan tradition, regeneration is the therapeutic healing in love that God seeks to offer. As part of God's salving and saving work, God both *declares us righteous* (justifying grace) and works to *make us righteous* (sanctification beginning in the new

---

7. Dean Blevins, "Catechesis and the New Birth: A Wesleyan Meditation," *Wesleyan Theological Journal* 53:2 (Fall 2018), 100.

birth) in a healing maturity of holy love. So what role does baptism play in these wonderful gifts?

Justification and the New Birth

Remember that baptism is the *ordinary* occasion where God offers pardon, forgiveness, and assurance. These gifts of God also seek and empower our continual response to grow in sanctifying grace as part of our ongoing healing.

Wesley affirmed that the new birth and justification occur at the same time (at baptism for infants and ordinarily at baptism for adults). This emphasis underscores the co-operant nature of salvation in the Wesleyan tradition. As initial justification pardons our sins, it also empowers and elicits our response "to the gracious further regeneration of our human faculties in the new birth."[8] This is another aspect to Wesley's evangelistic soteriology: "The new birth commences further co-operant transformation of our lives, empowered by sanctifying grace."[9] In other words, justifying grace invites a response that allows and invites the broader healing of initial sanctification in the new birth and beyond to commence. Although God's forgiveness can occur on many occasions when we confess and repent, the church affirms that at baptism there is a unique healing of God offering the full forgiveness of sins, and the fullest healing of God's justification, where God declares us righteous. At baptism, the old dies, and new life emerges.

Wesley celebrates that one of the benefits of baptism is "the washing away the guilt of original sin, by the application of the merits of Christ's death."[10] Later in Wesley's life and writing he was concerned that the transmission of the guilt from original sin might seem to deny our responsibility. Maddox notes that later Wesley writings suggest-

---

8. Maddox, *Responsible Grace*, 170.

9. Maddox, *Responsible Grace*, 170.

10. Wesley, *Treatise on Baptism*, II:1.

ed "human guilt was cancelled *at birth,* as one benefit of Christ's redemption."[11] The justifying grace that God offers at baptism does not mean such justification is *only* offered at baptism, but in an *ordinary* sense, it is the fullest declaration of God's initial justification.

As we have discussed already, Wesley allowed that, on occasion, God offers justifying grace at the Lord's Supper, depending on the need of the person.[12] Such grace offered at the Table does not mean the justification offered at baptism was incomplete but that baptism's justifying grace may need to be fully remembered and declared again in a discipleship journey. I have met people who have loved Christ for decades, but for a variety of reasons, they enter a phase when they feel overwhelmingly unworthy that God would forgive sins they committed long ago. They begin to drown in guilt and sometimes shame. A new and fresh encounter of justifying grace, declaring again God's pardon and forgiveness, becomes a balm and means of grace for people experiencing this doubt. The Eucharist is to be for all a continual renewal of the baptismal covenant that imparts justifying grace and enables a response into the new birth.

Regeneration as the New Birth at Baptism

While John Wesley never wavered on the importance of baptism as a means of grace, Randy Maddox notes that John Wesley's celebration of what occurs at baptism *did* shift. One of these shifts surrounds the degree to which adoption and the new birth as initial sanctification occur at baptism, either necessarily or at all.

The pietist evangelical voices in Wesley's life claimed that the new birth included a robust testimony of assurance of our adoption by God. This certainty was influenced by Wesley's own lack of assurance earlier in his life. Wesley

---

11. Maddox, *Responsible Grace,* 75.
12. Wesley, "June 28, 1740," *Works of John Wesley: Journal Diaries II,* 19:159.

negotiated the distinction by identifying some as having the "faith of a servant" (those who had been baptized and were church members) and others as having the "faith of a son" (those who could testify to their assurance of God's adoption).[13] After Aldersgate, Wesley connected the Spirit's work of adoption to those who were granted conscious assurance. Wesley's pastoral situation certainly guided his concerns. The challenge in England included the masses who had been baptized, often as infants, but were not living a present, vibrant, transforming faith.

Not only did Wesley become hesitant to celebrate adoption at baptism automatically, but he also eventually expressed doubt that the new birth was necessarily experienced at baptism. In his sermon "The New Birth," Wesley separates new birth and regeneration from the baptism experience, claiming that the sacrament of baptism offers the *outward* and visible sign of water that points to the *inward* and spiritual grace of death to sin and new birth in righteousness—but he felt that the inward transformation was not necessarily automatic.[14] These distinctions shape a maturing Wesleyan view of the sacraments. While God's gifts of adoption and regeneration are certainly offered at baptism, the importance of a full flourishing of adoption and regeneration require the human, God-empowered response.

Wesley was saturated in a culture where folks simply pointed to having been baptized and thought that was all God desired to do, while failing to respond to God's healing action. Wesley's pastoral burden was to necessitate that the outward sign of getting wet was to be joined to the inward healing God offered that demanded and empowered a human response for the full healing to flourish. Hence,

---

13. Maddox, "Introduction to Wesley's Treatises," *Works of John Wesley*, 14:246.

14. Wesley, "Sermon 45: The New Birth," *Works of John Wesley*, 4:1.

Wesley invited people to see that a deeper healing of the sacraments required a continual response to the healing God desires to do. These considerations Wesley made clear were for adults only.

What is intriguing is that, in the very next paragraph in the sermon "The New Birth," he notes that, for infants, the new birth and baptism are always linked. Infants at baptism *are* born again.[15] Because infants can't respond immediately, God's promise of being born again is assured, but since adult believers can respond, they may or may not testify right away to the assurance of adoption and new birth. Wesley's pastoral concern "did not focus on the absence of the Spirit's presence but on his hearers' lack of responsiveness to that presence."[16] Wesley celebrated baptism as the ordinary occasion of the new birth while also affirming that God was not restricted only to that occasion.[17]

Theologically and pastorally, this is all a bit of a mess. Within the deep pastoral desire for a vibrant and living faith and a robust testimony of assurance, it is yet problematic to regulate adoption as dependent on experiencing God's assurance. The importance of responding to God's healing and the gift of assurance cannot be denied, but it creates problems to separate what is happening for infants from what happens to adults. Moreover, it is deeply problematic to make one's own testimony of assurance the test as to whether one has been adopted by God. There are myriad reasons that adults may be unable to testify to such assurance. There may be trauma or cognitive or emotional or any number of other barriers preventing such testimony.

Admiring and following after John Wesley does not mean we ignore that a theological problem remains. He is

15. Wesley, "Sermon 45: The New Birth," *Works of John Wesley,* 4:2.

16. Maddox, *Responsible Grace,* 218.

17. Maddox, *Responsible Grace,* 250.

right to affirm the significance of assurance but wrong in his denial of adoption and new birth to anyone who cannot testify to that assurance. By way of analogy, infants or young children who are adopted into new families would not fully understand or comprehend their adoption at that moment, yet we would never say they are *less* adopted than a teenager who fully grasps the significance of their adoption.

For our purposes here, a strong Wesleyan theology of baptism celebrates that God not only unites us to Christ's death and resurrection, but also initiates us into the church, adopts us as children of God, and makes us born again by water and the Spirit, offering us regeneration as part of initial sanctification. This sacramental emphasis of God's faithful word and promise are assured. However, it is also essential that we continually respond to God's grace in order to experience the full healing into a vibrant faith that God desires to do through the sacraments. Moreover, the healing of the sacraments is not defined to one moment but is an ongoing healing that we are encouraged to let flow continuously. Baptism must always be imagined as a *beginning* of discipleship and not an ending.

Maddox notes that Wesley's *Treatise on Baptism* was written in 1756 to clarify his sacramental evangelicalism. The excerpt from the *Treatise on Baptism* quoted earlier celebrated the link between adoption and regeneration. Drawing upon John 3:5, Wesley notes that, "by *water* then, as a means, the water of baptism, we are regenerated or born again; whence it is also called by the apostles 'the washing of regeneration.'"[18] It is noteworthy that similar language appears in the Church of England's Article of Religion XXVII: Of Baptism.[19] In his sermon "The Marks of the New

---

18. Wesley, *Works of John Wesley: Treatise on Baptism*, 14:284, §2.4.

19. See Church of England, Article of Religion XXVII: Of Baptism, https:// www.churchofengland.org/prayer-and-worship/worship-texts-and-resources /book-common-prayer/articles-religion#XXVII. "Baptism is not only a sign of

Birth," Wesley celebrates that being born again of water and the Spirit is ordinarily part of one's baptism. Later, the importance of the human response also rose in emphasis for Wesley. Mental assent was not enough; a vibrant, true, living Christian faith is "a disposition, which God hath wrought in his heart, 'a sure . . . confidence in God, that through the merits of Christ, his sins are forgiven, and he reconciled to the favour of God.'"[20]

After his Aldersgate experience, "Wesley had come to see new birth in terms of a conscious conversion experience. This meant for him that baptismal regeneration could not be presumed past childhood. So becoming a Christian involved a born-again experience that was not marked by external ceremony or rite but was a life-transforming personal experience."[21] Wesley's own struggle for assurance and his pastoral concern for a present, dynamic faith among many in England who had ceased responding to God's healing initiatives caused a firm conviction of a sacramental vibrancy grounded in God's action but requiring and empowering an ongoing response. In this way Wesley celebrated dynamic *sacramental* encounters coupled with continual responses of pious conversion. It is telling that the liturgy for the baptism of infants that Wesley gave to the church in the young colonies of North America toward the end of his ministry celebrates the work of regeneration, new birth, and adoption:

---

profession, and mark of difference, whereby Christian[s] . . . are discerned from others that be not christened, but it is also a sign of regeneration or new birth, whereby, as by an instrument, they that receive baptism rightly are grafted into the church; the promises of forgiveness of sin, and of our adoption to be the [children] of God by the Holy Ghost, are visibly signed and sealed; faith is confirmed, and grace increased by virtue of prayer unto God. The baptism of young children is in any wise to be retained in the church, as most agreeable with the institution of Christ."

20. Wesley, "Sermon 18: The Marks of the New Birth," *Works of John Wesley,* 1:3.

21. White, *The Sacraments in Protestant Practice and Faith,* 70.

We call upon thee for this infant, that he, coming to thy holy baptism, may receive remission of sins for spiritual regeneration.[22]

Give thy Holy Spirit to this infant, that he may be born again, and be made an heir of everlasting salvation, through our Lord Jesus Christ.[23]

For adults, the need for God-empowered human response was necessary for the full vibrancy of the new birth at the waters of baptism.

Baptism as Icon of an Ecclesial Soteriology

To drink deep of the marrow of a baptismal imagination, we see the emphasis on God's first movement of salvation always wooing and empowering our response. In addition, one of the gifts of a baptismal emphasis is the celebration that salvation in the Christian tradition is thoroughly ecclesial. The good news of Christian salvation is embodied in our identity as reconciled to God, ourselves, and others. To find salvation is to find oneself as part of the martyr church, the body of the crucified and resurrected Christ. Saint Cyprian notes that one cannot find salvation to God that is also not connected to the church. For those trying to find salvation away from the church, Cyprian has these words: "He is a stranger; he is profane; he is an enemy. He can no longer have God for his Father, who has not the church for his mother."[24] Salvation is more than "just Jesus and me." A union with Jesus is also and always a union in the martyr church. This ecclesial center of salvation does not deny the personal response but actually makes it possi-

---

22. Wesley, "The Ministration of Baptism of Infants," *Sunday Service,* 140.

23. Wesley, "The Ministration of Baptism of Infants," *Sunday Service,* 141.

24. Cyprian, "Treatise 1: On the Unity of the Church," *Ante-Nicene Fathers* Vol. 5, ed. Alexander Roberts, James Donaldson, and A. Cleveland Coxe, trans. Robert Ernest Wallis (Buffalo, NY: Christian Literature Publishing Co., 1886), §6, https://www.newadvent.org/fathers/050701.htm.

Wesleyan Sacramental Theology

Wesley was far more pastoral than theologically systematic. Wesley scholars look at his own development and contextual responses, often referencing early, middle, or late Wesley according to the way he adjusted his thinking based on his experiences. This malleability has resulted in Wesley scholars having a difficult time making conclusive and consistent statements of some of Wesley's positions. A faithful Wesleyan theology of baptism today celebrates the glorious mystery of baptism as part of the beautiful tapestry of God's healing salvation into holy love.

ble. Sin works to separate and isolate individuals. Salvation is union and reconciliation in love in the body of Christ.

A Wesleyan theology of baptism celebrates a union with Christ's death and resurrection, which is therefore initiation into the martyr church and adoption as a child of God. Baptism grounds a Wesleyan celebration of salvation as ecclesial and affirms that at the covenant of baptism God offers initial justifying grace and the new birth as initial sanctification. God's offering of such gifts is not restricted to the age of the baptized. However, whether the believer is baptized at two months or twenty-two years, they must continually respond to God's healing acts initially offered at baptism in order to receive the full fruitfulness of God's grace. This necessity to respond is always empowered by God. Grace is about God all the way through, yet God's actions are not coercive, and the believer's continual response is necessary for the ongoing life of holy love. Baptism must always be seen as a beginning that provides the ground from which a life of joyful maturing in love can occur. By way of analogy, my wife and I made serious vows at our wedding. The ceremony and the day itself mattered because they set up the need for our daily embodied renewal of those vows as our marriage grew and matured. Likewise, a Wesleyan celebration of baptism can affirm the promise of God's work at the moment of baptism while also celebrating the ongoing daily response to let that healing flourish.

Baptized into the Priesthood

To be initiated into the martyr church as the body of Christ, one's covenant of baptism is not simply about one's own salvation but also celebrates a commission to live into the vocation given to all Christians. Just as Christ's baptism launched his public ministry, our covenantal salvation also ordains us for ministry in the world as the priesthood of all believers.

Sadly, the terms "laity" and "clergy" have often been used to create unhelpful divisions in the body of Christ. The laity are the priesthood of all believers. Martin Luther affirmed that our union with Christ in baptism is connected to our calling to be priests to the world: "For whoever comes out of the water of baptism can boast that he is already a consecrated priest, bishop, and pope. . . . We are all priests of equal standing."[25] Of course, context matters. James White clues us in that Luther's polemical comments pushed fiercely against the Roman Catholic Church in his day: "In 1520, Luther is proclaiming a radical equality on the basis of baptism, overturning all ecclesiastical status. This is as radical as it gets."[26] Luther felt mandated to challenge the harsh division between clergy and laity, and rightfully so. However, while laity and clergy are equal in status, just like 1 Corinthians 12, they do have different gifts and functions in the body of Christ.

A crucial celebration of the Protestant Reformation is that all Christians are Spirit-empowered to serve a priestly ministry in the world, loving, caring, shepherding, interceding, and praying for all others they encounter. Being baptized into the priesthood of believers as a lay member is a powerful vocation with great responsibility (see 1 Peter 2:9). In baptism, "through union with Christ, Christians continue his work in the world by signifying the love of God for the benefit of others. This is both the highest privilege of the baptized and the deepest responsibility. . . . Thus, his body on earth is the priestly community, the church."[27] Aidan Kavanagh notes, "The church baptizes to priesthood; it ordains to episcopacy, presbyterate, and

---

25. Martin Luther, "To the Christian Nobility of the German Nation Concerning the Reform of the Christian Estate," trans. Charles M. Jacobs and James Atkinson, *Luther's Works* Vol. 44 (Philadelphia: Fortress Press, 1966), 129.

26. White, *The Sacraments in Protestant Practice and Faith*, 59.

27. White, *Sacraments as God's Self Giving*, 117.

diaconate."[28] From the baptized laity, some are ordained as clergy for leading and organizing the church. There is no hierarchy between lay and clergy, only a discerning of the gifts in the church. There is no place in the church for clericalism—the assumption that clergy are the "real" or "most important" Christians. The professionalization of ministry is similarly problematic when it leads lay members to imagine all ministry should be done by clergy, "since we pay them to do that evangelizing and hospital visitation stuff."

All persons are baptized into the lay ministry of the priesthood of all believers. This baptism into the office of laity must always be imagined as a gift and intertwined into the gift and healing that are offered at baptism. The laity-clergy division has been a challenge in the church for more than a millennium, if not longer, but there is hope that, little by little, progress is being made across the Christian traditions. The church must emphasize the sacred gift and calling of all Christians into the priesthood of all believers in the lay vocation. Clergy must be more faithful to empower laity while also instructing and equipping lay ministry by the Spirit.

Baptism and Justice

Along with being an occasion for initiation into the church, baptism is a key event for justice in the church. White contends that baptism "is the sacrament of equality."[29] In Galatians 3:26–28, Paul celebrates the equality in the church as Christ's body: "You are all God's children through faith in Christ Jesus. All of you who were baptized into Christ have clothed yourselves with Christ. There is neither Jew nor Greek; there is neither slave nor free; nor is

---

28. Aidan Kavanagh, *The Shape of Baptism: The Rite of Christian Initiation* (New York: Pueblo Publishing, 1978), 188.

29. White, *Sacraments as God's Self Giving*, 113.

Wesleyan Sacramental Theology

One of the most divisive issues in the global church is the denial of ordination of women by some traditions. On this point the Wesleyan tradition has been clear in its *theology*, and is making progress in its *practice*, to celebrate God's calling and equipping of women for clergy roles of administration, leadership, oversight, and preaching. James White presses against traditions that deny women ordination: "Churches that refuse ordination to women, if they were consistent, would also deny their baptism. Anyone who is baptized in the general ministry ought to be considered a possible candidate for ordained ministry."[30]

---

30. White, *Sacraments as God's Self Giving*, 117.

there male and female, for you are all one in Christ Jesus." Paul makes clear that this equality is in the context of baptism. It is not a forced uniformity that erases our distinctions but an equality of beautiful diversity that we also see celebrated at Pentecost.

The categories Paul uses in Galatians 3 are examples of status markers that made it easy in his ancient context to elevate or demean people. By naming these markers, he is affirming that the baptismal waters drown and put to death all of our mechanisms for thinking some humans have more or less value than others. James White finds Hans Dieter Betz to be helpful in connecting baptism to justice and declared equality for all. Galatians 3:26–28 could serve as a powerful liturgy for baptism. This liturgy would form and instruct the newly initiated while also reminding those already baptized of the equality within the church. The liturgy would reiterate for the baptized "their eschatological status before God in anticipation of the Last Judgment and also inform them that this status affects, and in fact changes their social, cultural, and religious self-understanding, as well as their responsibilities in the here-and-now."[31] In baptism we find our identity in the crucified and resurrected Christ as members of the church, the body of this Christ!

Baptism is a covenant made between God, the church, and the person seeking to be baptized. I have known many individuals who have been attending church all their life but never been baptized. One could say those persons are simply "dating" Jesus and the church. Baptism is a full marriage into the covenant community. Baptism fully initiates us into the martyr church—the body of Christ.

---

31. Hans Dieter Betz, *Galatians: A Commentary on Paul's Letter to the Churches in Galatia*, Hermeneia (Philadelphia: Fortress Press, 1979), 184.

EIGHT | Faithful Baptismal Practice in the Local Church

I am a fifth-generation member of a denomination that is part of the pan-Wesleyan family where the importance of baptism has waxed and waned for a variety of reasons. My denomination has been impacted by the sacramental reformation of the late twentieth and early twenty-first centuries across Christianity, resulting in more baptisms performed now than perhaps ever in our hundred-plus-year history. Yet there is needed conversation about faithful pastoral baptismal practice that is part of a more robust sacramental discipleship of faith.

As a pastor, it has been my experience that most Christians in my denomination view baptism as nice but do not intentionally remember the sacrament as indelibly marking them by the Spirit with an identity in the body of the crucified and resurrected Christ. Within the Wesleys' dual sacramental and pietist passion, my tradition has often emphasized the piety of personal experience and conversion at the expense of God's sacramental activity. This error has led to several pastoral practices that undermine the divine power and ecclesial imagination of the Christian faith. My wise pastoral student Sam Bartolome has named the reduction this way: "Too often baptism in local churches feels more like a hazing ritual that gets one access to a country club of comfortable complacency rather than a covenantal initiation into the death and resurrection of the body of Christ."[1] Our theology shapes our practice, and our practice also shapes our theology. Practices are powerful and therefore need to be given careful and intentional consideration.

This chapter is an invitation into faithful baptismal possibilities and imaginations that can lead to a more robust identity in the martyr church. It is likely that many laity and perhaps even clergy have not been fully trained in faithful baptismal practices that draw upon the full breadth of our rich Christian tradition. As such, some readers may discover exciting new possibilities in baptismal pastoral practice while also lamenting past practices that may now appear less than ideal. The goal of this chapter is not to induce guilt for things done in the past but to inspire fresh and faithful baptismal celebrations. These recommendations for faithful baptismal practice are not exhaustive but will hopefully serve as a beginning for exciting and robust observations of baptism in the local church. All these practices draw upon the central theology of baptism articulated in the previous chapter.

Essential Baptismal Practices

Although there is room for some diversity in baptismal practice, there are also essential elements that should appear in every baptism ceremony. Christian baptisms must, at the very least, include water and be performed in the triune name. Additionally, it is ideal if they take place in public, communal worship and are performed by ordained clergy, but as we will discuss, leaving room for flexibility in extenuating circumstances or unique contexts is also possible.

---

1. Personal correspondence, June 20, 2022.

Water

Because Christian baptism has its Jewish roots with John the Baptist in the Jordan River, water has always been central to the celebration of baptism. God takes the ordinary element of water and infuses it uniquely with divine presence as a means of grace. Water represents death, new life, and cleansing. The church would not recognize a dry baptism. John Wesley celebrates the symbolic significance of water: "The matter of this sacrament is water; which, as it has a natural power of cleansing, is the more fit for this symbolical use."[2] Celebrating cleansing and new birth with an element other than water, such as mud, or flour, would be confusing and thus make a poor symbol.

Many Christian traditions offer the gift of baptismal fonts. Churches that have fonts near the sanctuary entrance encourage Christians to dip their hands in the water and place their wet hands on their foreheads to remember their baptism and affirm their identities as they come into worship as those marked by the bleeding yet resurrected Lamb of God.

Triune Name

Along with the universal use of water, baptizing in the name of the Father, Son, and Holy Spirit is another essential element that marks Christian baptism. The scriptural foundation is found most clearly in the Great Commission of Matthew 28. It is also important to note that baptism in the triune name is baptism into the one, holy, catholic (by which we mean universal, not Roman Catholic), and apostolic Christian church.

Triune baptism anticipates the full hope of the new creation kingdom where all creation will be caught up in the divine dance of love (*perichoresis*). Even as the ancient

---

2. Wesley, *Works of John Wesley: Treatise on Baptism*, I.2.

church wrestled with what it believed about the divinity of the Spirit, it still had the longstanding practice of baptizing in the triune name. Including the Spirit in baptism eventually encouraged the church to affirm the Spirit's divinity.[3]

Our practices shape our imaginations, which embody the ground of our beliefs, and those beliefs continue to shape our practices. Practice is the truest expression of belief. In the Christian tradition this truth is demonstrated in the link between the church's worship and doctrinal affirmations, formally known within liturgical theology as *lex orandi, lex credendi*: the law of prayer guides and guards the law of belief. God transforms the church in worship that impacts the church's beliefs. As the church reflects on this transformation it can also lead to further transformation of communal worship practices.[4]

Public, Communal Worship in the Local Church

The church has adjudicated that private home baptisms are not the best practice to celebrate one's initiation into the church. Because baptism is a covenant with God, it is also a covenant a local church makes to help love, care, nurture, and help mature in love the newly baptized. This recommendation does not preclude churches from performing baptisms in rivers or even private pools—*if* such celebrations include the full local church. However, in the twenty-first century, it is recommended that celebrating these sacraments in the context and physical space of the local church's ordinary communal worship is best. If a church does not have a baptistry, there are many creative alternative options. Full immersion is also not the only val-

---

3. For one example see St. Basil's *On the Holy Spirit*.

4. Two resources describing the relationship between worship, belief, and ethics as part of *lex orandi, lex credendi* are Aidan Kavanagh's *On Liturgical Theology* (Collegeville, MN: Liturgical Press, 1992), and Kevin Irwin's *Context and Text: A Method for Liturgical Theology* (Collegeville, MN: Liturgical Press, 1994).

id practice, in which case only some type of vessel to hold water would be required.

Although public, communal baptism in the context of the ordinary worship service is the ideal recommendation, there are exceptions when a person cannot physically come to the local church's communal worship. In such cases, the clergy and congregation should make the effort to bring as much of the church as possible *to* the baptismal candidate. It is a faithful baptismal practice to bring the communal worship service to those who are unable to attend ordinary worship.

I recall summer camps or weekend spiritual retreats during my tenure as a youth pastor when students expressed a desire to be baptized *at* those events. Often these students were responding to God's call on their lives, and they, like the Ethiopian eunuch Philip encounters in Acts, wanted to be baptized in the specific places where they felt God's call in order to seek God's further healing and deep initiation into the church. I love this passion and desire—but I wonder if something is missed when the fullness of the local church, beyond the youth group, is not present to be part of this covenant of mutual responsibility and ongoing care. This would also be true for children's events and the large variety of adult retreats. This is an area perhaps worthy of careful reflection.

Ordained Clergy

The sacrament of baptism ought to be performed by an ordained member of the clergy. God raised up the Levites among the twelve tribes of Israel to lead in their worship services. Similarly, clergy are called from among the laity for leadership in the church. The importance of the clergy in performing the sacraments comes down to the *order* of Christian tradition God has established. The clergy are trained, equipped, and empowered for certain roles in the church, including the celebration of the sacraments.

John Wesley affirmed the broad Christian tradition when it came to clergy involvement in the observance of sacraments, "arguing that it is proven by 'our Lord's commissioning his apostles only—and those who should derive their authority from them—to baptize.'"[5] This is the ideal, ordinary, and best practice.

The Roman Catholic Church set a precedent for emergency situations, declaring that the non-ordained *can* perform a valid baptism in the triune name with water, but this rationale is not shared by most Protestants. During the Middle Ages, midwives in the Roman Catholic context were empowered to baptize if they delivered an infant who did not have a strong chance of survival. The Roman Catholic tradition believed any unbaptized person (including infants) was in danger of hell. Most Protestants, especially Wesleyans, do not believe unbaptized infants will go to hell. Yet there may be occasions when a clergyperson is not able to get to someone who wants to be baptized or whose baptism is sought by someone else on their behalf. This exception should only cautiously be performed. For example, parents who want to baptize their own children at home as some sort of special family bonding experience would be considered outside the bounds of faithful sacramental practice.

Discrepancy in Tradition

For Protestants, the centrality of water and the triune name have served as the bare minimum. Other parts of Christianity include other rubrics for what they consider essential to a valid Christian baptism.

In 2022, a Roman Catholic priest was discovered as inadvertently not speaking the precise baptismal liturgy as prescribed in the Roman Catholic faith. Father Andres Arango, a Roman Catholic priest in Arizona, performed thou-

---

5. Wesley, *Treatise on Baptism*. Quoted in Maddox, *Responsible Grace*, 251.

sands of baptisms declaring "*We* baptize you in the name of the Father, Son, and Spirit," rather than saying "*I* baptize you . . ." as he poured the holy water over those he was baptizing. Thomas Olmsted, the presiding bishop with responsibility over Father Arango, concluded that, because the wrong words were spoken, all of Father Arango's baptismal services over the last twenty years were rendered invalid.

The Roman Catholic reasoning is that Christ alone mediates the sacrament through the priest, which is why it is important for the priest to say "I," acting as Christ in the performance of the sacrament. Conversely, saying, "We baptize" suggests all the church together is doing the baptism. The investigation concluded that Father Arango did not act with intent to harm, but the diocese determined that everyone who thought they had been baptized by him needed to resubmit themselves for baptism in order to be considered a baptized believer.[6]

Many Protestants, especially evangelicals, may find this issue to be a bit silly. However, Protestants should pause and reflect concerning the importance of being faithful to one's tradition and showing respect and care for sacramental liturgies. For Protestants, baptizing with water and in the triune name mark the event as Christian baptism. Without those essential elements, baptisms have not occurred.

Mode of Baptism

Water and the triune name are required for Christian baptism, and performing the sacrament in communal worship by ordained clergy is the *ordinary* recommended

6. Natacha Larnaud, "A Priest used one wrong word during baptisms. The church now says thousands were invalid," CBS, February 15, 2022, https://www.cbsnews.com/news/catholic-priest-andres-arango-baptisms-invalid-phoenix-church/.

practice. When it comes to the *mode* of baptism, though, the broader Christian tradition has much more flexibility.

Most Christian traditions affirm a variety of modes that can be employed. John Wesley also celebrated a variety of modes: "Baptism is performed by washing, dipping, or sprinkling the person, in the name of the Father, Son, and Holy Ghost, who is hereby devoted to the ever-blessed Trinity."[7]

Pouring water symbolizes the Spirit being poured out on all the people of God (see Acts 2:17).

Sprinkling with water connects to being cleansed through the sprinkling of Jesus's blood upon us (see Hebrews 12:24; 1 Peter 1:2, NIV).

Immersion in water is a powerful symbol of putting to death the sins we have done and the sins that have been done to us and being born again of water and the Spirit (see John 3:5).

Many Christian traditions recognize and accept as valid all of these modes of baptism. Although individual pastors may have their personal preferences, it is important to be sensitive to the needs of baptismal candidates. There may be people who, for a variety of reasons, have loved Jesus and been part of a local church for decades but have never been baptized. Perhaps they are even open and willing to being baptized but carry a great deal of shame and anxiety over not having been baptized. There are many reasons that seasoned Christians may not have been baptized, but we will look at a select few here.

Fear of Water

My denomination affirms and celebrates all modes of baptism, but the most common is immersion. That is often the only mode many in my denomination have seen, since

____

7. Wesley, *Works of John Wesley: Treatise on Baptism*, I.2.

we only recently recovered the practice of infant baptism. Pastors should be aware that there may be Christians who have not been baptized because they think immersion is the only way to do it and they are afraid of being dunked. Pastors would do well to talk about and offer a variety of modes as well as extend generous hospitality in guiding individuals into the unique mode that would be the most helpful for their faith journey.

Lack of Emphasis

Some Christians may have been following Jesus for a long time but were discipled in churches that did not emphasize the importance of baptism. My denomination, in its first seventy to eighty years of existence, certainly celebrated baptism but more strongly emphasized one's personal conversion through the sinner's prayer as the most important practice in the life of a believer. As such, there are many in my denomination who have loved Jesus and the church for a long time but have never been baptized. Some, after becoming aware of baptism's importance, feel embarrassed, guilty, or ashamed that they have not been baptized, so they keep their status silent and do not seek it out.

Pastors would be wise to emphasize that there is no shame in not having been baptized yet, and there is nothing to feel guilty or embarrassed about. Instead, we should invite with joy and excitement anyone who has yet to be baptized, helping them understand it is a failure of the church where they were improperly discipled as a Christian, not a personal failure of their own. It has been my distinct joy to baptize many parishioners in their seventies and eighties who have been part of the church with a deep devotion to Jesus for a long time.

Accessibility

I have also baptized several wheelchair users with pouring and sprinkling. When a sacrament is made visibly accessible to all, more people will want to participate, especially if our past practices have communicated, whether explicitly or implicitly, intentionally or otherwise, that it is only available to the able-bodied. It has been a cause for great joy for me to celebrate accessible baptisms at the front of the sanctuary where it is visible to all.

Infants, Believers, Dedications, and Rebaptisms

Another crucial area needing attention for faithful baptismal practice, especially in the evangelical tradition, surrounds infant baptism versus believer's baptism, baptism versus dedication for infants and young children, and requests for rebaptism. Both theologically and in practice, all of these issues are connected. As a pastor and professor, I have seen how these issues have become a swirling hornet's nest where the church is not always in agreement with itself. This unfolding discussion will be directly expressed within a Wesleyan sacramental theological framework.

Certainly, the Wesleyan tradition does affirm the importance of the human response, empowered by God, to God's grace for sacramental fruitfulness. However, too often baptisms among Wesleyan evangelicals have focused on the work or testimony of the person's response to God, rather than celebrating the work God will be doing in the baptism. Whether intentionally or unintentionally, some evacuate God from the sacrament by failing to celebrate God's salvific action in baptism.

The Wesleyan tradition is clear that God is at work preveniently healing *before* baptism, but there is also a unique salvific work God offers *at* baptism that is not replicated in any other practice. The broader Christian tradition, and specifically the Wesleyan tradition, asserts that those who are unbaptized miss out on central aspects of the salvation God desires to do in us as part of the unfolding of new creation.

Wesleyan Sacramental Theology

The Wesleyan tradition boldly celebrates God as the primary actor in the sacraments. God's activity is first God's presence (grace) wooing, inviting, and offering transformation both personally and ecclesially.

Moreover, baptism is how we encounter the reality that Christian salvation is thoroughly ecclesial. This theological foundation is crucial for the upcoming considerations.

Infant Baptism or Believer's Baptism? YES!

One of the most contested issues around sacramental practice is *when* a person should be baptized. Many Christians celebrate the baptism of infants, but some prefer to practice only believer's baptism, which simply means that someone is only baptized after they confess their sin and seek the salvation made possible through Jesus Christ. Some Protestants resist infant baptism only because it was initially a Roman Catholic practice. A more mature objection expresses the concern that infant baptism removes an individual's choice, discounting the need for their own response to God. This concern is both legitimate and unnecessary. Children raised in the church will often only know the love of the church and Jesus. For example, I never had a specific conversion moment. I was always just *in*. Just like with my biological family, my choice was not whether to *join* but whether to stay or to leave. Those who experience a believer's baptism must keep responding to God's grace all through their lives. Those who are baptized as infants should later go through a catechism program and publicly reaffirm their baptism once they have a greater understanding of their own faith journey. Baptizing infants celebrates that those children are God's and can thus live into baptismal grace at an early age.

John Wesley affirmed and celebrated infant baptism. His concern was not with when a person had been baptized but whether those who had been baptized had a dead faith or a vibrant, dynamic faith. Regardless of when people were baptized, Wesley wanted to know how they were living into God's baptismal grace *today.* He said in his *Treatise on Baptism* that "infants are capable of making a covenant, and were and still are under the evangelical covenant. The custom of nations and common reason of [hu]mankind prove that infants may enter into a covenant, and may be obliged by compacts made by others in their name, and receive advantage by them."[8] In this way, infants can be brought into a covenant they did not choose, just as they did not choose to be born, but later in life they must decide whether to live into that covenant.

John Wesley finds scriptural support by noting Jesus's command not to prevent the little children from coming to him:

> Infants are capable of coming to Christ, of admission into the church, and solemn dedication to God. That infants ought to come to Christ, appears from his own words: "They brought little children to Christ, and the disciples rebuked them. And Jesus said, Suffer little children to come unto me, and forbid them not; for of such is the kingdom of heaven" (Matthew 19:13, 14). Saint Luke expresses it still more strongly: "They brought unto him even infants, that he might touch them" (18:15).[9]

God desires children from the beginning to be marked by the Spirit in God's new creation covenant in the martyr church:

> God would never have made a covenant with little ones, if they had not been capable of it. It is not said children only, but little children, the Hebrew word properly signifying infants. And these may be still, as they were of old, obliged to perform, in after time, what they are not capable of performing at the time of their entering into that obligation.[10]

---

8. Wesley, *Works of John Wesley: Treatise on Baptism,* §IV:3.

9. Wesley, *Treatise on Baptism,* §IV:6.

10. Wesley, *Treatise on Baptism,* §IV:3.

Moreover, as Wesley recognizes, while baptism functions salvifically, the very practice of initiating infants into the Jewish covenant with God provides an important witness:

> But the apostles baptized infants, as is plain from the following consideration: The Jews constantly baptized as well as circumcised all infant proselytes. Our Lord, therefore, commanding his apostles to proselyte or disciple all nations by baptizing them, and not forbidding them to receive infants as well as others, they must needs baptize children also.[11]

Those who affirm believer's baptism only point out that there is no explicit mention of infants being baptized in the New Testament. However, Wesley also noted that, on Pentecost, families were baptized, and specifically in Acts, the jailer's whole household was baptized. Wesley recounts Peter's command at Pentecost: "Repent and be baptized, every one of you, in the name of Jesus Christ for the forgiveness of your sins. The promise is for you and your children" (Acts 2:38a, 39a, NIV).[12]

Wesley also recalls the broad history of the church that has overwhelmingly baptized infants. This encouragement to baptize infants does not deny the importance of their response to God's healing initiatives as they grow and mature. But with a good Wesleyan sacramental theology, this empowerment to respond to God's grace offered at baptism celebrates that God always offers healing first and that humans are continually invited to respond to it.

Rob Staples summarizes some key points for a Wesleyan celebration of infant baptism. While the guilt of Adam's sin is canceled at birth because of prevenient grace, one is born again at infant baptism. Prevenient grace is not origi-

---

11. Wesley, *Treatise on Baptism*, §IV:7.
12. Wesley, *Treatise on Baptism*, §IV:8.

nally offered at infant baptism, but it is certainly *proclaimed* and *illuminated* there. Baptized infants must be nurtured in the faith as they mature. They are then empowered to respond to the healing God offered first at baptism but that continues to be at work within each person as they respond to it. Failing to respond can lead to deliberately rejecting the healing God has offered previously in one's life. This reality honors that God's grace must always be responded to—not simply at the moment of baptism but all throughout one's life. A failure to respond well to God's healing work can lead to a person missing out on the fullness of salvation, and the healing is then thwarted.[13] The consequences of a failure to respond is true for baptized infants or adult believers and anyone in between.

One danger of affirming only believer's baptism is that it can privilege the human response to the work of God over the work of God itself. Infants, on the other hand, have done nothing—and indeed *could* do nothing—to earn or deserve the gift of God's grace offered at baptism. Infant baptism celebrates that God first chooses us. It does not deny the necessity of reaffirming the covenant made on their behalf, but it affirms the active salvific work in the life of the baptized infant, which also empowers their response all along the way. Parents, godparents, and the local church are making the covenant for this child in infant baptism on the infant's behalf. This acknowledgment is part of the pledge the community of faith proclaims to help rear and nurture this child into a faith formation that would lead to their later decision to reaffirm their baptism. Christian traditions with longstanding celebrations of infant baptism ordinarily do not baptize infants if there are not parents or godparents who are also baptized and who pledge to do this faith nurturing.

---

13. See Staples, *Outward Sign and Inward Grace*, 186–90.

There is absolutely a place in the church for believer's baptism as a present response to God's invitation to salvation, but the church should not deny access to God's salvific healing of little children. It is essential for churches to provide a robust catechism for all children, and it is especially important for children who were baptized as infants to be given the opportunity for a public reaffirmation of their baptismal covenant (see Appendix A). Those who are reaffirming their baptism should be dressed in white robes along with those receiving the sacrament of baptism, and they should also give their testimony celebrating their desire to reaffirm the covenant they were initiated into. When churches fail to practice appropriate liturgical observances of reaffirmation, there is little imagination for infant baptism and often too little resistance to rebaptizing.

Rebaptism? No! Reaffirmation? Yes!

Pastorally, I have been blessed to serve parishioners who were baptized as infants, teens, and adults who, for a variety of reasons, fell away from God and the church for a season. In their return to faith, they often want to mark their decision to come back into the body of Christ. Recall the parable of the prodigal son in Luke 15. When the younger son returned, he was welcomed back *as* a son. In the father's eyes, he was always a son even when he was far away. Baptized individuals who walk away from the body of Christ and then return can and should reaffirm their baptismal covenant in order to publicly celebrate the power of God's grace that never gave up on them. Remember God is the primary actor in baptism. To rebaptize is to indicate God's work was not quite good enough the first time. When baptism erroneously focuses on the human response, commitment, and testimony over God's action, people can become confused about the need to be rebaptized.

Rob Staples mentions H. Orton Wiley, who asserted that rebaptism is not a faithful sacramental practice and should not be done:

> Baptism being an initiatory rite is to be administered only once. It establishes a permanent covenant and is not therefore to be repeated. The baptized one may fall away, but the gracious promise of God still stands. It cannot be made of none effect. If he [or she] falls away, he needs to repent and believe, and the Father stands ready to restore him [or her], but he [or she] does not need to be rebaptized.[14]

Although rebaptism is to be avoided, testimonies and renewals of commitment to God are appropriate as many times as someone feels led to do so. The church can offer a liturgy of reaffirmation for those who walked away but later responded to God's call and invitation to return. Reaffirmation can be done by any believer as often as it is helpful in the journey, but especially those who drifted away for a time and adolescents who are reaffirming the covenant that was made for them in infant baptism.

It may be necessary for pastors to discern moments in which denying someone a rebaptism could do more harm than good. Most people who are unaware of the possibility of reaffirmation are very willing to participate that way once they have been offered appropriate theological and pastoral counsel. However, I once had a member of my church in his eighties who had been baptized during World War II at a camp in the Pacific. He wanted to declare again, in front of his local congregation, his continual desire to submit to God and follow God until the end of his life. As I listened to his story, I recognized that a theological exposition on why it is best to avoid rebaptism was not going to

---

14. H. Orton Wiley, *Christian Theology* vol. 3 (Kansas City, MO: Beacon Hill Press, 1940), 167.

connect with this man, and I supposed that in fact, a great wound could be inflicted by refusing the request. In the end, we did baptize him again, but I altered the traditional prayer as I immersed him. I said something like, "We celebrate Jim's* baptism again in the name of the Father, Son, and Holy Spirit." The rubric here is not simply to bow the knee to whatever the believer wants to do but to discern when pastoral care requires a more flexible response, as opposed to a rigid legalistic posture.

One final caution surrounds sentimental or tourist baptisms. As trips to the Holy Land have become more prominent for Christians, many tours include time at the Jordan river. Some become eager to be baptized in the same river where John baptized Jesus. While I have no doubt such an experience would be meaningful, such an event should include a liturgy of reaffirmation for those who are already baptized. We must remember the sacraments come to us as a gift and are not our playthings to consume and use in any way we desire. Yes, they can and should be fun and joyful and life-giving, *and* they are also holy actions to be done with care and discipline.

The Dedication of Infants and Young Children

During the middle era of my denomination's history, our sacramental theology was guided immaturely by the insistence that we are *not* Roman Catholic. This posture encouraged many liturgical and sacramental practices to be avoided not on theological grounds but simply on the petty reasoning that such practices were too close to Catholicism. This avoidance included not only sacramental apathy but also limited observance of the full Christian calendar. Many evangelicals expressed great resistance to baptizing infants. As such, some traditions invented a ritual of dedication as an alternative option to infant baptism. While some attempted

*Not his real name.

to ground such practice in the scriptural narrative of Hannah and Samuel (see 1 Samuel 1:21–28), the notion of dedication on its own is a historically recent invention—one that, ironically, seems to take its cue from the liturgies of infant baptisms, where parents and godparents and the local church make the covenant on behalf of the infant and promise and pledge to raise the child in the faith.

Although the practice of offering children to God is wonderful, these rituals are not sacramental because the church is not asking anything from God. Those who are dedicated as infants instead of baptized are expected to be baptized at a later age after they have participated in baptismal catechesis. In his book *Outward Sign and Inward Grace*, Rob Staples offers some important pastoral cautions about the danger of confusing infant baptism with infant dedication. Along with him, I strongly suggest no water of any kind be used in a dedication ceremony. It is perhaps fine to give a flower and a Bible to the infant and their family, but appropriate pastoral teaching will clarify the distinctions between dedication and baptism.

For those wondering whether pastors should encourage families toward baptism or dedication, elders should always make it clear that both options are acceptable and available. Infant dedication is not *more* right than infant baptism, and infant baptism is not wrong. There should always be clear and precise teaching on the differences between infant baptism and dedication.

Catechism

The sacramental revolution and recovery of important practices, especially among evangelicals in the last thirty to forty years, has meant a rise in the number of baptisms performed in denominations and churches that have historically been sacramentally apathetic. As a sacramental theologian and pastor in one such denomination, I have embraced this transformation as the bountiful blessing that it is, but along with that joy come words of caution. Church history provides some helpful guidance for the process of baptism.

In church tradition, baptism was preceded by a long, intentional process of catechism (teaching, instruction, discipleship formation). Some early Christian churches had a catechism process of up to three years. This season of formation was not about assessing a person's worthiness but about inviting them to humbly submit themselves to church discipline and practice. Along this journey were mentors and sponsors who helped to guide these *catechumens*—Christian converts seeking to be baptized.

In churches in the twenty-first century, too many pastors feel guilt or perhaps even disinterest about requiring even thirty *minutes* of instruction, let alone three years. Properly viewed, baptism as an act of initiation into the church is not a right that is *owed* to anyone who does or does not do the required (or recommended, as the case may be) amount of work beforehand. Nobody *deserves* to be baptized. The church determines whether a candidate is ready for baptism or if an infant's parents and/or godparents will faithfully raise the child in the church. Baptism is best imagined as the church *letting you in*. Baptism is not a *right* but a gift offered by God as discerned by the Spirit in the life of the church.

When Christianity is imagined as a personal trek with Jesus, it becomes too easy to disregard the necessity of the church. All local churches should facilitate a robust, intentional catechesis for children and for adults who have converted to the faith. This time of instruction is about formation into the full breadth of the Christian covenant. It is also advisable that people of all ages have a sponsor or mentor who can journey with them during catechism and beyond to the celebrations of baptism and reaffirmation.

Although there is no longer a fixed or set amount of time for catechism, simply asking baptismal candidates to show up thirty minutes before the baptismal service is bad pastoral practice. In my local church, our children's department spends about three months in weekly intensive instruction with many pastors and teachers journeying with our sixth graders. I have also found that two to three months of weekly classes supplemented with home reflection is helpful with adults. Some churches do have a much lengthier process of formation that they find transformative. The season of Lent had its roots in preparing persons for baptism. The church found the process so helpful that they recommended the entire church celebrate this season every year in preparation for the Easter season.

Spontaneous Baptisms

A few baptismal practices do fall outside faithful observance. I have been in a few churches that had spontaneous baptismal services. Rather than calling people to the altar, these churches would call people to a small body of water as a response to God's movement in the worship service. These churches had gathered extra changes of clothes and towels ahead of time so nobody would be precluded from participating if they were not prepared in regard to clothing. Viewing baptism in this way leads to a devaluing of the work of God. It also tempts pastors to present baptism as something that is "fun" and "cool" instead of sacred and significant. In these services, first-time baptisms were as common as rebaptisms, which encourages Christians to view the sacrament as dependent on whether we've had a good or bad week individually, rather than something that depends entirely on the grace of God meted out in the context of the universal church. I can affirm that the churches I observed doing this only had the best of intentions, but this particular method falls outside the bounds of faithful baptismal practice.

Baptism is a covenant in addition to being a sacrament. I like to ask my students if any of them wants to get married *today* to anyone else in the class, especially someone they barely know. They all laugh, although there are always a few guys who pause just long enough that it can get a wee bit uncomfortable. Of course, the idea of spontaneous marriage is silly. Even in traditions and cultures that practice arranged marriage, the process is careful and deliberate, not spontaneous. Therefore, since the baptismal covenant is even more serious and significant than the marriage covenant, spontaneous baptism should be avoided. There are, as usual, seeming exceptions. Someone who suddenly decides to be baptized after being part of the church for decades is not actually making a spontaneous decision but one that is a result of their many years being formed by the church. Like the couple who get "spontaneously" married after dating for ten years—it was time.

Final Thoughts on Faithful Baptismal Theology and Practice

This chapter is far from comprehensive. There are many other important rubrics and suggestions for faithful baptismal practice. Let me offer a few summary ideas from the last two chapters, along with a few simple best practices.

1. **Teach and preach and practice a robust theology of baptism.** It is likely that most churchgoers know what baptism is (although some may not), but everyone will benefit from regular teaching about its full hope and promise. This teaching and preaching should include:

    a. Naming the unique Wesleyan theology of baptism that proclaims a union in Christ's death and resurrection, initiation into the martyr church, adoption into the family of God, and salvific healing of justification and initial sanctification of regeneration, or new birth.

b. Guiding the church into understanding the distinctions between infant and believer's baptism, and how infant dedication is wonderful—but not a sacrament.

c. Confirming both the importance of the sacrament of baptism and the needed, ongoing response to God's grace that is empowered by God and supported by the local congregation.

d. Celebrating the importance of reaffirmation for those baptized as infants and also as a meaningful ritual for those coming back to faith who may think they need to be rebaptized.

2. **Develop a strong catechesis**. Such programs should be both for those seeking baptism and those who want or need to reaffirm their baptismal covenant.

3. **Encourage the use of sponsors or mentors**. Those seeking to reaffirm their baptismal covenant or receive the sacrament of baptism should always be guided and journeyed with by someone more mature in the faith.

4. **Celebrate the sacrament of baptism all year—but especially on Easter Sunday and Pentecost as a blessing of the new birth.** By example, discourage those who think there are more important things to do in communal worship on these high holy days than observing and celebrating the sacraments.

5. **Use white robes for new baptismal candidates as well as those who are reaffirming their baptism.** The white robes symbolize God's cleansing and healing.

6. **Draw upon the rich liturgies of the church.** Appendix A has an example of a baptism liturgy that has its foundation in the *Book of Common Prayer* with a few adaptations. The liturgy includes space for the baptism of infants and adults and a ritual of reaffirmation, as well as an invitation

for all who have been baptized to renew their baptismal covenant.

7. Encourage all Christians to find their deep identity in the crucified and resurrected Jesus Christ. Baptism into the martyr church is initiation into the life, death, and resurrection of Christ. Those who are baptized ought to be vigilant against all other temptations for citizenship, loyalty, and allegiance.

8. Be creative and have fun while drawing upon the deep baptismal traditions of the church! Sacraments are serious and significant, but that doesn't mean they have to be somber and funereal.

NINE

The Sacrament of Eucharist

If the sacrament of baptism is how God grows the church, then the Lord's Supper is the meal of ongoing sustenance for the continual transformation of Christians into the image of Christ and a continual renewal and re-membering of the martyr church.

Although only one baptism is needed, the Lord's Supper is the meal *of* the baptized that sustains the martyr church and offers continual healing in sanctifying grace. In the Lord's Supper it is important to recognize the importance of presence, the union of **oblationary** (an act of praise and thanksgiving) sacrifice, and that the church is renewed to be sent out as the broken, crucified, and resurrected body of Christ in the world.

The Eucharistic Means of Grace

John Wesley saw the Lord's Supper as a primary sacrament of the church.[1] All the **works of piety** and **works of mercy** culminate in this celebration. The Lord's Table is a foretaste of the eschatological feast of the new creation. The full hope of the new creation celebrates the cosmos caught up within the triune dance of love. The eucharistic meal is a triune transforming encounter that both anticipates the new creation feast and works to help bring it more fully to

---

1. See Wesley, "Sermon 16: The Means of Grace," *Works of John Wesley*, 1:381, §II.1.

earth as it is in heaven. While in the ordinary sense, baptism is the sacrament of initiation, initial justification, and the new birth, so too is the Lord's Supper the sacrament of sanctification. Yet also recall John Wesley's certainty that God offers preventing, justifying, or sanctifying grace at the Lord's Supper according to the need of each person. Christ's presence at the Table, by the power of the Spirit, from the will of the Father, meets each person where they are on that journey, inviting and wooing them into the healing of holy love as part of the martyr church.

This healing is simultaneously personal and ecclesial. Just as baptism helps frame a Wesleyan view of salvation as thoroughly ecclesial, so too is the Eucharist a means of grace that seeks to heal and transform individuals as part of the larger martyr church. This ecclesial emphasis grounds our ongoing healing and maturation of love in Christlikeness. The healing and transformation God is working is part of further irruption of God's new creation breaking forth. Moreover, it also reminds me as an individual that, as I navigate my spiritual journey as part of the martyr church, I am not satisfied with my own growth in holiness if my sister or brother is struggling. Although there can be dangerous levels of unhealthy enmeshment where boundaries are lost, we are ultimately meant to be what Cain did not understand: our brother and sister's keeper. As the body of Christ, we are expected to more deeply journey together through life's joys and heartaches (see Romans 12:15).

Because the sacrament of sanctification is an ongoing journey, there is always more depth to the maturity of love. Like the apostle Paul, we never fully attain it but press on to allow God to keep moving us toward the goal of holy love for God, ourselves, one another, and creation (see Philippians 3:13–14).

The remainder of this chapter will deal with three of the central aspects of a celebration of the Lord's Supper:

presence, sacrifice, and mission. Both presence and sacrifice have historically created points of great division in the church, but we will look at them through a Wesleyan lens. As with baptism, the goal is never to exhaust the mystery but to iconically lean into the great gift God has offered the martyr church.

Presence

In the Protestant Reformation a great deal of consternation and ink were spent disagreeing about Christ's presence in the Eucharist. The issue of presence not only pertains to Christ's presence but also to how the people—the body of Christ—are present. John and Charles Wesley unequivocally affirmed that Christ was present in the Eucharist. While Wesleyan scholars have not come to clear consensus as to which Reformer they most closely align with, I suggest that the Wesleys' position breaks new ground by moving away from a *science* of the presence to one of affirmative mystery. For the Wesleyan tradition I have named this celebration of Christ's presence at the Table as a "doxological mystery."[2]

The Wesleys reflect on the glorious mystery of Christ's presence at the Table in *Hymns on the Lord's Supper*. "Hymn LIX" draws on a passage from Daniel Brevint describing the joyful mystery surrounding Christ's eucharistic presence by allegorizing the Gospel narrative of Jesus healing the blind man: "Indeed in what manner this is done, I know not; it is enough for me to admire. *One thing I know* (as said

---

2. In other places, most specifically my book *Created to Worship*, I have used the term "doxologically agnostic." At its root, the term "agnostic" refers to people who believe things cannot be known. Moving forward, the word "mystery" better captures the spirit of the Wesleys' position.

the blind man of our Lord), *he laid clay upon mine eyes, and behold I see.*"[3] The Wesleys affirm in this corollary hymn:

God incomprehensible
Shall man presume to know,
Fully search him out, or tell
His wondrous ways below?
Him in all his ways we find;
How the means transmit the power
Here he leaves our thoughts behind,
And faith inquires no more.

How he did these creatures raise
And make this bread and wine
Organs to convey his grace
To this poor soul of mine,
I cannot the way descry,
Need not know the mystery,
Only this I know, that I
Was blind, but now I see.[4]

This hymn captures well the spirit of doxological mystery. I reflected in *Created to Worship*: "While not exhausting the mystery of the manner of Christ's presence, mystery leads to worship—doxology. This hymn proclaims that God reveals all things necessary for healing, namely being seen by and then *seeing* Christ. Somehow the eyes of people are opened so they are seen by Christ and see Christ, which describes all the illumination needed."[5]

Although John Wesley affirmed Christ's presence, he was not enthusiastic about defining Christ's presence regarding substance (a metaphysical ontology). The Scho-

---

3. Brevint, *Christian Sacrament and Sacrifice* in Rattenbury, *Eucharistic Hymns*, 151, §IV.3.

4. Wesley and Wesley, "Hymn LIX," *Hymns on the Lord's Supper*, emphasis added.

5. Peterson, *Created to Worship*, 178.

lastic language of eucharistic substance was not clear in
Scripture, and perhaps, in Wesley's pastoral wisdom, he
thought discussions and arguments about substance and
species would rob the Eucharist of its central emphasis—
the healing encounter with Christ.[6] Therefore, any discussions
with an agenda to define whether Christ is bodily or
spiritually present *in* or *around* the elements simply is unhelpful.
Borgen concurs: "Wesley needs neither a doctrine
of ubiquity nor a philosophy of 'substance' and 'accidents'
to explain this mystery."[7] The Church of the Nazarene
celebrates the Lord's Supper as "a means of grace in which
Christ is present by the Spirit."[8] This emphasis on Christ's
presence is central to a Wesleyan celebration of the Lord's
Supper, keeping the focus pastoral without an overreach of
the mystery.

Discussions about Christ's presence in the Eucharist
often miss the work of the Holy Spirit, not only in making
Christ present but also in helping make *Christians* present
to God and to one another. The United Methodist **epiclesis**
in the "Great Thanksgiving" eucharistic prayer petitions
the Father, "Pour out your Holy Spirit on us gathered here,
and on these gifts of bread and wine. Make them be for us
the body and blood of Christ, that we may be for the world
the body of Christ, redeemed by his blood."[9] Note the
petition for the work of the Holy Spirit to transform not
only the bread and juice but also *us*—those who partake of
the eucharistic elements—to become the body and blood

---

6. For a further explanation of the scholastic positions on Christ's presence,
including how the terms "substance" and "species" are understood, please consult
the glossary.

7. Borgen, *John Wesley on the Sacraments*, 185.

8. Church of the Nazarene, *Manual: 2017–2021*, "XIII. The Lord's Supper,"
34–35.

9. United Methodist Church, "Word and Table Service: Thanksgiving and
Communion," *The United Methodist Hymnal: Book of United Methodist Worship*
(Nashville: United Methodist Publishing House), 10.

Wesleyan Sacramental Theology

In the Eucharist, Christ is present by the Spirit, but the Spirit also makes the body of Christ (the church) present for a divine-human transformative encounter.

of Christ. The issue of presence is not simply how is Christ present but also how we are present in order to become Christ's body and blood. The great Augustinian celebration in the Eucharist affirms that *we become what we receive* (the body and blood of Christ).[10]

Sacrifice

Another point of concern among the Reformers was the notion of the Lord's Supper as a sacrifice. The Wesleys were intentional to celebrate the sacrificial nature of the Eucharist.[11] Celebrating the Lord's Supper as a sacrifice does not suggest Christ's work on the cross is insignificant or needs repeating. Rather, as Christ continues to offer himself by the Spirit at the Lord's Supper, in the spirit of Romans 12:1–2, we offer ourselves back to God in thanksgiving. The sacrificial nature of Christ and ourselves is one of oblation—praise and thanksgiving.

For Wesleyans, there is a helpful illumination on the notion of sacrifice and holiness. The word "sacrifice" is formed from the two Latin roots *sacere* and *facere*. *Facere* means "to do or make." *Sacere*, "to be holy," is also where we get the English word "sacred." In this context, a central meaning of sacrifice is to do or make something holy—for Wesleyans, sanctification. At the Lord's Supper, the Holy Spirit makes Christians present to God and to one another and empowers us to offer ourselves as a living sacrifice. The Holy Spirit then renews and remakes us as the body and blood of Christ. This entire movement of God is a further healing in sanctification. The Lord's Supper is a feast of thanksgiving and celebration that offers us healing and re-members us as the one body and blood of Christ.

---

10. St. Augustine, Easter Sermon 227.

11. *Hymns on the Lord's Supper* has an entire section (#4) focused on the Lord's Supper as a sacrifice. Section 5 emphasizes "Sacrifice of Our Own Persons."

Mission

The Holy Spirit gathers Christians into communion for healing and restoration and sends us out to participate in God's mission in the world. Recall the Church of the Nazarene's eleventh Article of Faith: "The mission of the church in the world is to share in the redemptive and reconciling ministry of Christ in the power of the Spirit."[12] As the Holy Spirit breathes in the church for communion, the church is then breathed out by and with the Spirit to continue the work of God in the further inbreaking of the kingdom of God.

Communion in worship is a place for encountering God through scriptures read and proclaimed, which invites and empowers a human response through confession, praise, intercession, and lament (spoken and sung), culminating as often as possible in the Lord's Supper as a crescendo where the church is transformed and renewed as the body of Christ both communally and personally in their ongoing healing and transformation. This communion of communal worship then anticipates being sent out *by* and *with* the Spirit with a benediction to be Christ's body and blood in the world, moving the church out in doxological mission.

At baptism, all Christians are ordained by Christ into the office of the laity. Laity are the priesthood of all believers sent into the world to participate in God's kingdom coming more fully every day. The significance of this holy work leads to an important conversation about moving out from the Table into the world for God's mission.

---

12. Church of the Nazarene, "XI. The Church," *Manual: 2017–2021*, 33.

Excursus
The Holy Work of the Laity Participating in God's Kingdom Coming

In his book *Work Matters*, Tom Nelson has offered some helpful critiques and blessed invitations for how all Christians can engage in our ordained ministry throughout the week. Nelson laments that clergy training often lacks emphasis on empowering, equipping, encouraging, and sending out Christian laity to see their lives and work as ministry in the world. This oversight has resulted in a large gap between Sunday's worship and Monday's work. Specifically, Nelson charitably laments when the blessing at the end of a worship service only encourages the body to come back the following Sunday, describing such inadequacy as a failure of kingdom imagination and of the pastoral office to equip the saints for ministry.

Ephesians 4:11 describes the different ways God has equipped the body of Christ. The role of clergy is to give oversight and leadership to the church. Paul goes on to say that God's "purpose was to equip God's people for the work of serving and building up the body of Christ until we all reach the unity of faith and knowledge of God's Son. God's goal is for us to become mature adults—to be fully grown, measured by the standard of the fullness of Christ" (Ephesians 4:12–13). The focus and goal of helping to enact God's mission in the world is not that humans by our own work bring the kingdom but that God can unite us in the faith and knowledge of God's Son. Without over-stretching this passage, it seems plausible to interpret that ordained clergy are set apart to equip the laity for ministry, and through that work, God will bring both unity and knowledge of Christ.

With gracious and empowering insight, Nelson calls for a broader theology and blessing of work throughout the week. When Christians see the actions we do all week long as a contribution to and participation in the present and ever-coming kingdom of God on earth as it is in heaven—rather than simply a hobby to be enjoyed or a job to get money—we can reimagine how holy our work is in the world. The church must empower an imagination where our actions from Monday to Saturday are not separate from our identity as members of the body of Christ. How can we empower all—from the CEO of a large corporation all the way down to workers on the lowest rung on the ladder, across all fields of work and industry, and also those who do not work for a living or are not paid for the work that they do—to recognize that everything they do can and should be seen as holy work done in thanksgiving for all that God is doing? All Christians ought to view our Monday-to-Saturday activities—paid or unpaid, jobs or hobbies—as an opportunity to live out our vocation as members of the body of Christ. Our vocation is a calling that chooses us more than simply things we enjoy doing. A vocation is much more than fun self-actualization; rather, it is seeing our life and work offered to God as an act of worship and thanksgiving. This perspective undergirds the notion that God has a vocation, or calling, for all Christians in all corners of the world.

This emphasis also can help eliminate the unhelpful tendency toward sacred-secular dualism. There is no such thing as a "secular" job or activity. When Christians view everything we do as a holy-sacred participation in God's kingdom coming, whether it's the way we make a living or the way we spend our free time, we will begin to consciously and intentionally assess how fruitful our efforts in the world are, which may sometimes lead to re-prioritizing or reevaluating how we spend our time. Paul exhorts that *whatever* we find ourselves doing, we must do it all to the glory of God (see Colossians 3:17). This vision prophetically encourages us to be careful that what we do, whether in work or in play, does not form our central identity of meaning and value, over and against our identity as members of the body of the crucified and resurrected Christ. Even those in overtly Christian or ministerial contexts can sometimes become consumed with how we are building our own kingdoms for our own glory instead of focusing on building God's kingdom for God's glory.

I had the privilege in one of my general education classes of getting to know Ruth Ann, an adult student working to finish her undergraduate degree. Toward the end of the semester, she asked if I could meet with her and her husband, Lance. Lance had been an active member in the United States Navy with a job in electronic military intelligence and weaponry systems. Early in their marriage Lance started to feel unwell. At first the symptoms were minor, but slowly his condition worsened, and he ended up having to retire from the military. Lance was eventually diagnosed with a rare, brutal autoimmune disease. Although it progressed slowly, the disease robbed Lance and Ruth Ann of many dreams and plans. Soon Lance could not take care of himself, and Ruth Ann became his full-time caregiver, at which point I was blessed to be invited into their journey.

Ruth Ann was faithfully caring for Lance, but it was becoming more and more challenging, and they needed help. I invited them to my Sunday school class, which gave the other members of that class the opportunity to become not simply encouragers through prayer but also fellow laborers with Ruth Ann and Lance. As the years continued to roll forward, Lance continued on a slow but steady decline that included many ambulance trips to the ER and treatments at the VA, often with lengthy stays. Lance and Ruth Ann needed help with the holy work around the edges of their lives—mowing, deck-building, gardening, changing lightbulbs, shoveling snow, singing Christmas carols, playing board games, watching baseball, and making trips to see waterfalls, flower fields, and sunsets. Lance and Ruth Ann invited others into their holy work. It was not always easy. Some fellow laborers who meant well caused additional emotional strife and suffering. Ruth Ann had to become assertive in her holy work that occasionally led to some needed isolation.

This journey of work was long and sometimes torturous. Ruth Ann's work was holy, self-sacrificial, long-suffering—in short, it was *kenotic*. Yet it was not only Ruth Ann and this band of friends who were working; Lance was also working hard every day. His work was eating, doing puzzles, telling jokes, and speaking even when it became unbearably difficult. His work was choosing to live. While the joint work of friends was beautiful as the years continued to pass, Ruth Ann and Lance's patient work was nothing less than sacramental. Of course, it was not fun. It was hard, brutal, excruciating, unrelenting. With the work of the community suturing Lance and Ruth Ann with love, Lance's love for Ruth Ann and Ruth Ann's life vocation of caring for Lance as an act of love empowered Lance to live as long as he did. The work of extending Lance's life came not from a fear of death but from a calling to work to love each other. Like the work of many spouses who are caregivers, they worked daily to fulfill their marriage vows to love each other until *death us do part*. They could have chosen to give up, but they worked and worked and worked as an outflow of God's love. And one of the greatest gifts they both gave and received was allowing others into their work, which meant not only letting others complete tasks for them but also letting others play with them. On several occasions, they invited my young daughter to come over to paint and play games. It was a community of fellow laborers in the economy of God's love.

At one point Ruth Ann told me that she sensed Lance's journey in this life was coming to a close. I was teaching an evening class when I got a text from Ruth Ann that Lance had begun his final journey. I asked if she wanted me to come over as I had two nights previously to work by just sitting and singing with them. She said it was happening fast and that she was okay. Lance finished his work in this life about twenty-five minutes later. The news came simply, in a text. Lance's work in this life was finished.

I had the privilege of leading Lance's celebration of life. Family and friends gathered outside to recognize the work they had all co-labored together to do. We acknowledged Lance and Ruth Ann's work of mutually offering themselves to each other fully and deeply. One of the greatest gifts Ruth Ann and Lance gave many of us was the invitation into the joy of working together with them, and we were all able to watch as our work was woven together into a beautiful tapestry of love.

Ruth Ann's work in this life continued. For a long season, her work became resting, grieving, and recovering from the many years she had spent as a devoted caregiver. Today she works through photography, painting, and being close to family even as her work of grief continues.

Many other examples of holy work can be celebrated. The point is that all Christians are to be at work each day as an act of thanksgiving and joy for the life and healing God continues to offer. This labor from Monday to Saturday is then offered as a living sacrifice each Lord's Day in the inhaling, or gathering, of the members of the body of Christ. This communal worship of offering ourselves on the altar as a *living sacrifice* (see Romans 12:1) helps remind the body of Christ that this work must always be God's work and not our own that we attempt to possess and control.

Much more can and should be said about the importance of this holy work. Nelson's *Work Matters* is connected to his passionate belief that all Christians are *made to flourish.* Although it is important to avoid sacred-secular dualism, there is some work that we are to avoid such as work that destroys or works against the kingdom of God. Wisdom from the larger community can help Christians discern work that should and should not be done. Not only is there work to avoid, but Scripture is also clear about our obligation to participate in God's work to bring justice for all. To cite just one example of many: "He has told you, human one, what is good and what the LORD requires from you: to do justice, embrace faithful love, and walk humbly with your God" (Micah 6:8). Sometimes it is important to work without thought of monetary compensation. The Gospels are instructive in encouraging all Christians to give special attention and service *to* and *with* the most vulnerable in society: "True devotion, the kind that is pure and faultless before God the Father, is this: to care for orphans and widows in their difficulties and to keep the world from contaminating us" (James 1:27). This devotion is certainly a work of compassion while also keeping a keen eye out for work that goes against God's kingdom coming and our healing and flourishing in love. It is faithful to steward the resources of our time and work to explicitly care for the most vulnerable around us.

Christian work is doxological, and God invites our participation as co-laborers (see 1 Corinthians 3:9). Yet this work is always empowered and made possible by the power of the Spirit. God invites and empowers our participation as the continual working out of our own salvation. None of this work achieves or earns the compensation of God's healing. It is all about God's grace as a gift through and through, yet this work is part of how we can work out our salvation (see Philippians 2:12).

Some of the most important yet most neglected work that God commanded is sabbath. From Genesis all the way to Jesus, Scripture testifies to the importance of sabbath. It is important not to view observing sabbath as slothful.

Sabbath is the work of focusing and celebrating that God can be trusted to provide and care for both the lilies of the field *and* the workers in the field. Sabbath work is resting from the work of the week that tempts us to find alternative kingdoms and identities away from God and the kingdom of God. Sabbath work invites us to remember that our value and worth are not connected to producing more bricks with less straw. Sabbath work reminds us we are not God, and that God can be trusted to provide for God's creation. Sabbath contrasts with our regular work to remind us that all our work is always done as doxology and praise for all that God has done and is doing. This work we do in the week is not an attempt to compensate God. Our work during the week is the fruit of love that God continues to sow in us every day, and we allow it to flourish. From the sacrament of communal worship, our lives are to be sacramental—a means of grace to the world as we live Monday to Saturday.

Faithful Eucharistic Practice in the Local Church

TEN

Eucharistic formation is connected to a robust, historically grounded theology, but equally crucial is the intention and care we take in our Eucharist celebrations. This chapter will consider some recommendations for faithful practice through a Wesleyan lens. Connected to all these faithful recommendations and rubrics is the primary acknowledgment that God is doing something powerful and unique. God's invitation to transformation both elicits and empowers a human response that leads to sacramental fruitfulness and flourishing.

Many evangelical traditions, especially in the pan-Wesleyan family, have begun celebrating the Lord's Supper more frequently. Within this new eucharistic zeal, attending to the wisdom of Christian tradition can both guide a faithful connection to the past and inspire fresh yet faithful creativity. This chapter begins with a conversation around frequency, then who can preside over the Table and who can serve the elements. Then follows a discussion about what constitutes faithful elements and who can partake. Finally, we will consider proper preparation, prayer suggestions, and when Eucharist should occur in a local communal worship service.

The aim of this chapter is to offer resources for local churches that draw upon the rich marrow of the global church's eucharistic tradition. While each local church must do appropriate contextual work, remaining grounded in broader church tradition is encouraged.

Frequency

One of the important ecclesial issues for eucharistic practice regards frequency. How often should we partake of the Lord's Supper? The renewed zeal for this sacrament in evangelical Wesleyan traditions led to the question of whether the sacrament might somehow "lose its meaning" if it were practiced more often. Certainly there are many things in life where moderation is important and we can have too much of a good thing—like ice cream! I told my wife that, since things are more special when they are less frequent, I had decided to tell her I loved her only on the first day of the month. After all, it would be less special if I told her too often! As you might imagine, that did not go over well. It turns out there are many aspects of life where there is no such thing as "too much"—such as the love we have and express for our spouses and children.

The history for the Wesleyan family is important. The Methodist reformation has been rightly described as a sacramental reformation. Although John and Charles largely affirmed the existing Anglican eucharistic theology of their day, their zeal for regular practice was revolutionary. In his sermon "The Duty of Constant Communion," John implores a robust sacramental practice:

> We must neglect no occasion which the good providence of God affords us for this purpose. This is the true rule—so often are we to receive as God gives us opportunity. Whoever therefore does not receive, but goes from the holy table when all things are prepared, either does not understand his duty or does not care for the dying command of his Saviour, the forgive-

ness of his sins, the strengthening of his soul, and the refreshing it with the hope of glory.[1]

This call to regular participation celebrates the great healing God desires to do in those who partake as well as the way the meal re-members and re-unites the church as the body of Christ. Participation was so important for the Wesleys that they labeled it a "duty" of any Christian who desired to keep growing in the healing of holy love.

While John was helping set up the Methodist Episcopal church in the United States, he ordained Richard Whatcoat and Thomas Vasey and Thomas Coke. Coke was commissioned as a superintendent (a title equal with, and later changed to, bishop) to ordain Francis Asbury and others. These ordinations were irregular in the Church of England. For John, the importance of the Eucharist coupled with the tradition that ministers be ordained led to an important minimum in priestly celebration of the Eucharist. These ministers were charged in the United States to get to churches on their circuit at least once a quarter. There were so few ordained Methodist ministers in the United States at that time that quarterly Communion was as much as could be managed.

Unfortunately, the understanding of quarterly Communion as a minimum in service to sacramental passion was lost over time, and Communion observance once every three months became an inadvertent maximum. For two hundred years, John and Charles Wesley's sacramental passion was not able to cross the Atlantic to their pan-Wesleyan denominations. Fortunately, along with the broader sacramental revival, the pan-Wesleyan denominations began to recover their eucharistic zeal in the late twentieth

---

1. Wesley, "Sermon 101: The Duty of Constant Communion," *Works of John Wesley*, 3:429, §3. This sermon was adapted largely from Robert Nelson's 1707 sermon "The Great Duty of Frequenting the Christian Sacrifice."

century. This recovery has meant an increase in the frequency of observance, but there remains a great need for education about the dynamic gift of eucharistic theology and proper practice. Now that the Eucharist has become "cool," well-meaning pastors and congregations have engaged in practices that are less than ideal and fall outside the bounds of what can properly and faithfully be called Eucharist.

Weekly Eucharist is a wonderful rhythm, but no matter how often the sacrament is observed, it is crucial for a pastor to guide the congregation in a deeper education of what the Eucharist is and is not, seeking to provide a deeper level of engagement and transformation in the local church. The illumination of this dynamic means of grace can help offset the concern about an increase of frequency causing a loss of sacred character. As with all change, pastors will do well to help their local congregations process how and why an increase in frequency may occur. Remember that change equates to loss, so the process of decision-making is as important as, if not more important than, the actual decision itself.

Who Can Preside?

One of the important questions regarding a proper eucharistic celebration is who presides over the sacrament and consecrates the elements. On this point, John and Charles (along with most of the universal church) are crystal clear. In England during the Wesleys' lifetime, many laity had been commissioned to field preaching because of the growth of vibrant Methodist meeting houses. In addition, many Methodist meeting houses wanted permission to celebrate the Eucharist in their gatherings. John and Charles adamantly rejected their request for two reasons: First, to celebrate Communion in these Methodist meeting houses would be literally breaking communion (severing ties) with the Church of England. The entire Methodist movement was meant to be a revival movement *within* the Church of England, not an attempt to break away from the church. Second, John and Charles made clear that only the episcopally ordained had been given authority and empowerment to preside at the Eucharist Table.

Although John had stretched and strained the Church of England's polity regarding field and lay preaching, the Wesley brothers always upheld established tradition when it came to who could preside at the Table. The importance of ordination was the reason behind the once-quarterly minimum set for the circuit priests in the United States. During all those other weeks that an ordained member of the clergy was not there, a church could not receive Eucharist. Some will note that "breaking communion" with the Church of England shouldn't have been a concern since most priests in the Church of England had already broken from Roman Catholic apostolic succession. Regardless, the importance of the ordained is as crucial to good orthodoxy (right worship) as is baptizing with water in the triune name.

Some may wonder about parts of the globe where there are simply not enough ordained pastors and priests. Lamentable though these situations are, the solution is not to break with church tradition. Rather, denominational leaders should be creative about recognizing the authority of ordained ministers from other traditions and working diligently to ordain pastors who are already serving. Clergy are ordained for communal worship to empower the baptized laity to engage in their ministry all week long as part of the priesthood of all believers. That is the ministry of their holy work. However, a strong sense of egalitarianism also celebrates the great diversity of giftings in the church. Therefore, it would be inappropriate and unnecessary to become slothful regarding the importance of ordained clergy.

Ordained clergy are the only ones empowered by the Holy Spirit and given authority by the church to consecrate the elements. Later in this chapter we will celebrate the importance of a historical eucharistic liturgy. Some from the evangelical tradition have not always participated in the Great Thanksgiving prayers of the church. Some reduce their liturgies to what is called the Institution Narratives, largely from 1 Corinthians 11:24–25 or a compilation of Last Supper accounts from the Gospels. Most Great Thanksgiving prayers in the Wesleyan tradition include these narratives, but the larger prayer also contains many other wonderful elements.[2] One of those elements is called the epiclesis, which refers to the invocation of the Father to send the Holy Spirit during a eucharistic prayer. Here is the epiclesis from the liturgy provided in Appendix B:

> Pour out your Holy Spirit on us gathered here, and on these gifts of bread and the cup. Make them be for us the body and blood of Christ, that we may be for the world the body of Christ, redeemed by his blood.
>
> By your Spirit make us one with Christ, one with each other, and one in ministry to all the world, until Christ comes in final victory, and we feast at his heavenly banquet. Through your Son Jesus Christ, with your Holy Spirit in your Holy church, all honor and glory is yours, Almighty Father, now and forever.[3]

This specific prayer asking the Father, by the power of the Spirit, to transform the elements *as well as the church* into the body and blood of Christ has been affirmed by broader church tradition as something to be prayed by the ordained clergy. Just as we baptize in the triune name, the church has

---

2. See chapter 22 in Peterson, *Created to Worship,* for a more detailed conversation on all parts of the Great Thanksgiving prayer.

3. United Methodist Church, "A Service of Word and Table I: The Great Thanksgiving," *Book of Worship*, 38.

confirmed through the testimony of the Spirit that only the ordained (typically elders) have the authority and power to lead the congregation in this prayer.

Who Can Serve?

Presiding at the Table is different from serving at the Table. Best practice is for ordained ministers to serve themselves first, and then those who will be serving. Although it is often considered culturally polite to serve oneself last in other meal settings, the Eucharist is a special case symbolizing that Christians can only share what they have first received. Any member of the church can serve after the elements have been consecrated by an ordained member of the clergy. It is wise to be intentional with who is asked to serve. It is fitting for children, the old, the young, those who are economically poor and rich, those who are married or single, all genders, all ethnicities, etc., to serve. This consideration is not tokenism but an intentional acknowledgment and celebration of the fact that the Eucharist anticipates the heavenly feast where there will be people from every tribe, language, and tongue (see Revelation 7:9–17).

How to Serve?

How the Eucharist is served is deeply theological and can either transform persons into Christ's image or malform us away from the body of Christ. Considering how to serve Communion is always contextual. It is my preference to serve by intinction. Intinction often happens at the front where there is an altar, although there may be serving teams in multiple places around the edges of the sanctuary depending on the size of the congregation. Intinction usually consists of one server holding the bread and another the cup. Those receiving the Eucharist come forward toward the altar. Remember, every Lord's Supper is a sacrifice. While Christ continually offers himself, our coming to the altar symbolizes our presenting and offering ourselves to God. We come with our hands open and cupped because we never *take* Christ; we always *receive* Christ. The server holding the bread might say something like, "This is the body of Christ, broken for you" as they place the bread in the recipient's hand. The recipient then dips the piece of bread into the cup as the second server says something like, "This is the blood of Christ, poured out for you." Then the recipient partakes of the combined elements in that moment. It is important for churches that serve by intinction to be prepared to go to where people are sitting if there are people in a congregation who have limited mobility.

Intinction is preferable to serving people separate elements in pews with trays. Although it is theologically correct and beautiful to pass on to others what we receive, the symbolism of sitting in our seats rather than coming forward is more passive. Serving trays do add levels of efficiency and convenience, but whatever mode of service is used should have its significance understood and explained by the pastoral team. Some who are used to receiving the elements by passing them down the rows find it meaningful for everyone to take the bread together at the same time, and then for everyone to take the juice together at one time, usually following a pastoral leader's invitation, instead of what happens with intinction, where participants take the elements individually. For some, partaking altogether at the same time symbolizes unity in the church. The key for any pastoral team is to celebrate the Eucharist with intention and not simply do what is the easiest or most efficient. After all, what more important things do we have to do in communal worship than the sacraments?

When we serve Communion, we also need to remember who is not in the room. How are children included in eucharistic celebration? Many churches bring their children back from children's programming specifically for

Communion so they can partake as part of the congregation. But how do nursery workers get to partake? We must also remember those who cannot physically gather in the sanctuary. One of the historic roles of ordained deacons was to take the Eucharist elements to the homebound. The church has a duty to bring the church to those who cannot physically be in the sanctuary on a regular basis. This act of connecting and ministering to people in their homes was revived during the COVID-19 era in the form of new ministries that have continued beyond the pandemic.

Does Eucharistic Matter, Matter?

We have affirmed that water is essential in the sacrament of baptism. For the Eucharist, what are appropriate symbols for bread and wine? Bread and wine were common, ordinary things in the first century, widely available and easy to come by. It is God's good pleasure to take things that are common and transform them into powerful means of grace (God does this with humans as well).

The first Lord's Supper occurred during a Passover meal, which meant they had unleavened bread because Passover was not a feast but a meal to be eaten in haste in anticipation of a journey soon to follow. Conversely, the Eucharist as we now celebrate it *is* a feast, which means it can be long and slow and celebratory and does not require unleavened bread. The *Didache*: "As this broken bread was scattered over the mountains, and when brought together became one, so let your church be brought together from the ends of the earth into your kingdom."[4]

Similarly, human hands take the individual grapes that God grows and crush and press them together to form one vat of wine. Christians are the unique and scattered heads of grain and individual grapes. God gathers us,

---

4. *Didache*, in Jasper and Cuming, *Prayers of the Eucharist*, 23.

crushes and presses us together, and kneads us into one loaf and one common cup. This theology means that Doritos and Coke are simply not good bread and wine symbols.

As a practice of hospitality toward others, it is best to have gluten-free or other simple breads that allow for all to share from the same loaf. Another best practice concerns eucharistic elements that have not been consumed at the conclusion of the celebration. Any remaining elements should be cared for with reverence. Consecrated bread can either be safely stored for future services, or distributed and eaten after the service, or taken and served to members of the congregation who are prevented from coming to the communal worship gathering. Any leftover wine or juice can be drunk or poured out into creation. It is best not to simply throw the elements in the trash or flush them down the drain.

Who Can Partake?

On the point of who can participate in the Eucharist, the universal church is not in full agreement. At a basic level, it is largely affirmed across Christianity that the Lord's Supper is a meal of the baptized, but there are variations to this affirmation. The conversation of who can partake can be referred to as *fencing the table.* For the Roman Catholic Church, the Orthodox Church, and a few Protestant traditions, it is essential for those receiving Eucharist not only to have been baptized but also that their baptism and confirmation, if applicable, were performed in that specific faith tradition. Other Protestant traditions celebrate that the Lord's Supper is for the baptized but welcome all who are baptized, regardless of which faith tradition performed the baptism.

Wesleyans practice an open Table, the first layer of which means, for example, that a Roman Catholic or Episcopal or Baptist or Lutheran or Presbyterian believer who is

Wesleyan Sacramental Theology

Individuals are not baptized into a denomination but into the church universal.

baptized can attend a Methodist (or other Wesleyan tradition) service and be welcomed at the Lord's Table. Wesleyanism affirms the importance of baptism as the *ordinary*
requirement for the Table but also extends an invitation in
an *extra-ordinary* measure of hospitality to those who have
not yet been baptized but are open to and desire God's
healing presence to come and transform them. This position is taken from the example of Jesus's table fellowship in
the Gospels, which makes clear that sinners do not defile
the Lord's Table. God keeps inviting all who desire to come
and partake and have their lives transformed. This extra-ordinary invitation does not discount the central, ordinary
affirmation that the Lord's Supper is a meal of the baptized
for our ongoing growth in sanctification. Yet this extra-ordinary hospitality also honors that this partaking of the
Lord's Table could be a means of conversion to the faith in
a dynamic way.

Here is an example of a possible invitation to celebrate
both the ordinary and extra-ordinary invitation to the
Table:

> *Today we are humbled that God has opened up God's Table
> again to us, those who were once on the outside, who by
> our baptism have been brought into the covenant as God's
> children. Those who are baptized are invited to commune
> to reaffirm your baptismal covenant as God desires to offer
> fuller healing on your journey of sanctification. In addition,
> those who are not baptized but who desire God's healing
> and transformative power and presence in your life are also
> invited to partake as you offer all of yourself to God. May
> we become of what we partake—the body and blood of Jesus
> Christ as part of God's new creation kingdom coming more
> fully every day.*

This invitation both welcomes and offers instruction as to
the great mystery of grace God desires to work in this celebration. Within this extra-ordinary hospitality to those who

are not baptized, it is also critical that pastoral staff encourage those not yet baptized to strongly consider entering into the process of moving toward baptism. Pastors should also be aware that those from Roman Catholic or Orthodox traditions may come to the Table with their arms crossed. This simply means they do not want to partake but are seeking a short blessing from the minister.

What about Children?

Parents often wonder about when children should begin partaking. The church universal has a variety of practices on this issue. With the best of intentions, some may suggest that only those who can cognitively understand what is happening should partake. Although being consciously formed into the great teachings of the church is wonderful, important, and beautiful, this barrier is unwise. For Wesleyans, there should be no cognitive achievement required to partake of and encounter the grace of the Table. I have a PhD in the sacraments and with deep, serious affection, I still find myself awed and mystified by God's mystery of grace.

As a pastor, I work with parents to help guide their decision. My general recommendation is that any child who can physically eat the bread and drink the juice can partake. All humans have been fed and nurtured in ways we did not understand in our infancy, yet that nourishment was a blessing for a lifetime. It is a tremendous gift to the church when children only have memories of being welcomed to God's Table of love.

Another good practice connects to what words of blessing are said to a child in the Eucharistic celebration. In the weekly Word and Table service I lead, we have several young families who attend regularly. In one family, the parents attended before two of their three children were born. In consultation with the parents, we blessed their infants for a couple years before they decided it was time for their child to eat and drink as they were physically able.

Typically when serving the Eucharistic elements, the serving minister will say something like, "This is the body of Christ broken for you" when offering the bread and, "This is the blood of Christ poured out for your sins" when offering the cup. Young children are often concrete, literal thinkers, so hearing about eating a body and drinking blood can cause big eyes or fear and confusion. Not everyone finds it necessary to change what children hear at the Eucharist Table, but for those who do wish to be intentional with their wording toward children, there are several alternatives that can be offered, in consultation with parents.

I often say to children, "Take this bread and drink this juice to remind you that God loves you very much. I hope you know, [name of child], that you are loved by God and are very special to God." There are many other wonderful options that are shorter and can be said to worshipers of all ages: *the bread of life, the cup of salvation; the bread of heaven, the cup of love.* These are merely a couple of appropriate suggestions among many thoughtful and creative choices.

Caution about Feeling Unworthy

Scripture offers areas of consideration other than baptism pursuant to a proper preparation for Eucharist. One of the great blessings in my life has been participating in several global theology conferences within my home denomination, the Church of the Nazarene. One such conference was in Johannesburg, South Africa. In that gathering we were split up into groups from around the world. In one of our small group conversations focused on the Eucharist, I was surprised and saddened to hear about a regular practice in multiple African countries regarding participation in the Lord's Supper. Drawing upon 1 Corinthians 11:27–32, they interpreted these verses to mean that if they had any sin in their lives, they were unworthy and therefore could not partake of Communion so as not to bring condemnation upon themselves. These African siblings in the faith reported that many of their fellow parishioners rarely partook of Communion because of their guilt from sin. Hearing this story broke my heart. In the same vein as Wesley's ultimate rejection of the Moravian claim that only persons who had *assurance* should partake of the sacrament, Wesley was crystal clear that *none* of us are worthy—God invites and desires all to partake who are hungry and thirsty and in need of God's cleansing and transformative power.

This sentiment about fear of being unworthy was a problem Wesley faced in England as well. In his important sermon "The Duty of Constant Communion," he offers a clear command and admonition, asserting that the one who fails to commune is in danger of disobeying God.

> Fear it not for eating and drinking unworthily; for that, in St. Paul's sense, ye cannot do. But I will tell you for what you shall fear damnation: for not eating and drinking at all; for not obeying your Maker and Redeemer; for disobeying his plain command; for thus setting at nought both his mercy and authority. Fear ye this; for hear what his apostle saith: 'Whosoever shall keep the whole law, and yet offend in one point, is guilty of all.'[5]

The Wesleys, therefore, implored Methodists to commune as often as possible. First Corinthians 11 is focused on matters of hospitality and social justice. Paul was upset that the rich were communing and not waiting or leaving any gifts from the eucharistic table for the poor and those who came later from their daily labor. The unworthiness was not a matter of personal sin but a failure of justice for the economically poor

---

5. Wesley, "Sermon 101: The Duty of Constant Communion," *Works of John Wesley*, 434, §II.9.

Wesleyan Sacramental Theology
Faithful eucharistic practice is that every person who is open to God's healing and grace should be invited to the Lord's Table.

in their community. One is never worthy to commune, but God's invitation is especially for those who recognize their need for God's healing and transforming presence.

Perhaps the only scenario where individuals should not partake of the Eucharist would be those who know they are living in blatant sin and have no desire to repent. Yet pastorally, if a person is willing to have God soften their heart toward their sin, the Table should be open. The church must never forget that Christ extended his body and blood to Judas as well as eleven others who scattered and abandoned him later that same night. For those who desire to commune, God's grace can handle each complexity of their life.

Eucharist Liturgy

The Wesleyan tradition encourages its churches to draw upon the great eucharistic prayers of the church, often called the Great Thanksgiving. The *Book of Common Prayer* can be a wonderful resource for contemporary Wesleyans to use and contextualize for their local congregations. There is a sample liturgy in Appendix B that is grounded in the *Book of Common Prayer* (*BCP*). The *BCP*'s Great Thanksgiving has deep roots and connections to eucharistic praying that has occurred for millennia across all of Christianity. These prayers are not magic, but—just like the Lord's Prayer and the creeds of the church—they are a cherished resource for Christian worship and formation that connects Christians past, present, and future.

When in the Service Should Eucharist Occur?

Drawing upon the rich history and tradition of Christian worship, we follow the ancient pattern that the service of the Lord's Table follows the service of the Lord's Word. The Table is the culmination of the congregation's response to God's revelation in the scriptures read and proclaimed.

After prayers of confession and intercession, the giving of tithes and offerings to be placed on the eucharistic table, and confessing the creeds, God invites Christians to be present to Jesus in order to be further transformed into his body and blood.

Conclusion

Sacraments in the Wesleyan tradition are an ordained gift from God. Although God offers healing and transformation in many times and places, the sacraments of baptism and the Lord's Supper celebrate that being Christian is about being incorporated into the martyr church, the body of the crucified and resurrected Jesus Christ. In the sacraments, God offers healing and transformation to be set free from sin into a great depth of love. God offers God's transforming presence as grace, while also seeking and empowering our response to allow God's healing to flourish.

This healing is not just about the individual but is a fashioning and maturing of the universal church. The martyr church is the eschatological fruit of the new creation kingdom that is here yet also coming more fully each day. As God gathers the church in communal worship for our renewal as the body of Christ, we are then sent out to be about holy work as our doxology of praise. This is the work of the martyr church—the bride of Christ. Through this work, God invites us to participate in the continuing work of the incarnation.

May we drink deeply of the great gift of the marrow of God's transforming presence in order that God may indeed be all in all.

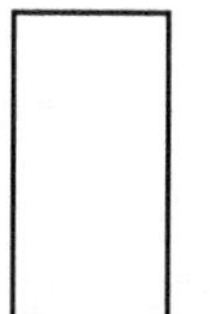

Appendix A:
Baptism Liturgies

This sample baptismal liturgy has been modified from the *Book of Common Prayer*. This collection of liturgies includes the baptism of infants and teen or adult believers, a reaffirmation of baptism for the already baptized, and a call for all who are baptized to renew their baptismal vows, so it can be modified and parts omitted or left in as appropriate for each context.

Invocation

In Ordinary Time
Pastor: Blessed be God: Father, Son, and Holy Spirit.
People: And blessed be his kingdom, now and forever. Amen

From Easter Day through the Day of Pentecost
Pastor: Alleluia. Christ is risen.
People: The Lord is risen indeed. Alleluia.

In Lent and on other penitential occasions
Pastor: Bless the Lord who forgives all our sins.
People: His mercy endures forever.

Pastor: There is one body and one Spirit;
People: There is one hope in God's call to us;
Pastor: One Lord, one faith, one baptism, one church;
People: One God and Father of all.
Pastor: The Lord be with you.
People: And also with you.
Pastor: Let us pray.

Presentation and Examination of the Candidates

Pastor: The candidate(s) for holy baptism will now be presented.

Adults and Older Children

The candidates who are able to answer for themselves are presented individually by their sponsors, and each sponsor's declaration is followed in turn by an individual question and response between the pastor and the candidate.

Sponsor: I present [NAME OF CANDIDATE] to receive the sacrament of baptism.

Pastor: Do you desire to be baptized?

Candidate: I do.

Infants and Younger Children

The candidates who are unable to answer for themselves are presented individually by their parents and sponsors.

Parent(s)/Sponsor(s): I/we present [NAME OF CANDIDATE] to receive the sacrament of baptism.

After all have been presented, the pastor addresses all of the parents and sponsors in a collective call-and-response liturgy.

Pastor: Will you be responsible for seeing that the child you present is brought up in the Christian faith and life?

Parents/Sponsors: We will, with God's help.

Pastor: Will you by your prayers and witness help this child to grow into the full stature of Christ?

Parents and Sponsors: We will, with God's help.

Pastor: Will you lead and nurture this child to embrace and affirm the covenant made on their behalf today?

Parents and Sponsors: We will, with God's help.

Affirmation and Reaffirmation

Pastor: The other candidate(s) will now be presented.

Presenter: I present these persons who desire to affirm and reaffirm their baptismal vows.

Renunciations and Profession of Faith

The pastor asks the following questions of the candidates who can speak for themselves, and of the parents and sponsors who speak on behalf of the infants and younger children, and of those who are affirming and reaffirming their baptismal covenants.

Question: Do you renounce all the spiritual forces of wickedness that rebel against God?
Answer: I renounce them.

Question: Do you reject the principalities and powers of this world that corrupt and destroy the creation of God?
Answer: I reject them.

Question: Do you repent of your sin and all desires that draw you from the love of God?[1]
Answer: I repent of them.

Question: Do you turn to Jesus Christ and confess him as your Savior?
Answer: I confess him.

Question: Do you put your whole trust in his grace and love?
Answer: I trust him.

Question: Do you promise to follow and serve Christ as your Lord?
Answer: I will follow and serve Christ.

Congregational Covenant

The pastor addresses the congregation.

Pastor: Those of you who witness these vows, will pledge to support these persons in their life in Christ?

People: We will with God's help.

---

1. This renunciation is also an act of consecration of one's life to the sanctifying work of the Spirit.

Pastor: With God's help will you proclaim the good news and live according to the example of Christ?

People: We will with God's help.

Pastor: Will you surround these persons with a community of love and forgiveness, that they may grow in their trust of God and be found faithful in their service to others?

People: We will with God's help.

Pastor: Will you pray for them, that they may be true disciples who walk in the way that leads to life?[2]

People: We will with God's help.

Pastor: We invite all those who have been baptized to stand and reaffirm your baptism. Let us join with those who are committing themselves to Christ and renew our own baptismal covenant.

Pastor: Do you, as Christ's body, the church, reaffirm both your rejection of sin and your commitment to Christ?

Baptized Congregation: We do.

The Baptismal Covenant

Pastor: I now invite the candidates for baptism, all those who are baptized, and any others who would like to profess their faith to stand.

Pastor: Do you believe in God the Father?

People: We believe in God the Father almighty, Creator of heaven and earth.

Pastor: Do you believe in Jesus Christ, the Son of God?

People: We believe in Jesus Christ, his only Son, our Lord. He was conceived by the Holy Spirit and born of the Virgin Mary. He suffered under Pontius Pilate, was crucified, died, and was buried. [He descended to the dead].[3] On the third day he rose

---

2. United Methodist Church, *Book of Worship*, 89.

3. This phrase is a later addition to some versions of the creed and may be omitted if desired.

again. He ascended into heaven and is seated at the right hand of the Father. He will come again to judge the living and the dead.

Pastor: Do you believe in God the Holy Spirit?

People: We believe in the Holy Spirit, the holy catholic church, the communion of saints, the forgiveness of sins, the resurrection of the body, and the life everlasting.[4]

Pastor: Will you continue devotion to the apostles' teaching and fellowship, to the breaking of bread, and to prayer?[5]

People: We will, with God's help.

Pastor: Will you persevere in resisting evil, and, whenever you fall into sin, repent and return to the Lord?

People: We will, with God's help.

Pastor: Will you proclaim by word and example the good news of God in Christ?

People: We will, with God's help.

Pastor: Will you seek and serve Christ in all persons, loving your neighbor as yourself?

People: We will, with God's help.

Pastor: Will you strive for justice and peace among all people, and respect the dignity of every human being?

People: We will, with God's help.

Prayers for the Candidates

Pastor: Let us now pray for these persons who are to receive the sacrament of new birth and initiation into the church [and for those persons/ this person who have/has renewed their commitment to Christ].

A person appointed leads the following petitions.

---

4. Pastors should take care beforehand to make it clear that "catholic" with the lowercase c refers to the church universal.

5. This is from Acts 2:42. In the original Greek, it is "prayers," plural.

Leader: Deliver them, O Lord, from the way of sin and death. Open their hearts to your grace and truth. Fill them with your holy and life-giving Spirit. Keep them in the faith and communion of your holy church. Teach them to love others in the power of the Spirit. Send them into the world in witness to your love. Bring them to the fullness of your peace and glory.

Pastor: Grant, O Lord, that all who are baptized into the death of Jesus Christ your Son may live in the power of his resurrection and look for him to come again in glory; who lives and reigns now and forever. Amen.

Thanksgiving over the Water

The pastor blesses the water.

Pastor: We thank you, almighty God, for the gift of water. Over it the Holy Spirit moved in the beginning of creation. Through it you led the children of Israel out of their bondage in Egypt into the land of promise. In it your Son, Jesus, received the baptism of John and was anointed by the Holy Spirit as the Messiah, the Christ, to lead us, through his death and resurrection, from the bondage of sin into everlasting life. We thank you, Father, for the water of baptism. In it we are buried with Christ in his death. By it we share in his resurrection. Through it we are reborn by the Holy Spirit. Therefore in joyful obedience to your Son, we bring into his fellowship those who come to him in faith, baptizing them in the name of the Father, and of the Son, and of the Holy Spirit.

The pastor touches the water.

Pastor: Now sanctify this water, we pray by the power of your Holy Spirit, that those here are cleansed from sin and initiated into the life of the church and may continue forever in the risen life of Jesus Christ our Savior. To him, to you, and to the Holy Spirit, be all honor and glory, now and forever. Amen.

Baptism

Each candidate is presented in turn, by name, to the pastor, or to an assisting helper, who immerses or pours water upon the candidate, saying:

Pastor: [NAME OF CANDIDATE], I baptize you in the name of the Father, and of the Son, and of the Holy Spirit. Amen.

When this action has been completed for all candidates, the pastor, at a place in full sight of the congregation, prays over them.

Pastor: Let us pray. Heavenly Father, we thank you that by water and the Holy Spirit you have bestowed upon these your servants the forgiveness of sin, and have raised them to the new life of grace and initiated them into the church. Sustain them, O Lord, in your Holy Spirit. Give them an inquiring and discerning heart, the courage to will and to persevere, a spirit to know and to love you, and the gift of joy and wonder in all your works. Amen.

Pastor: Let us welcome the newly baptized. The peace of the Lord be always with you.

People: And also with you.

Appendix B: Eucharist Liturgy

This sample eucharistic liturgy draws on the *Book of Common Prayer*, the United Methodist Great Thanksgiving, and the author's own liturgical amendments.

Preparation for Holy Communion

Pastor: The Lord's Supper was ordained by God to be a means of conveying grace according to the need of each person. No preparation is indispensably necessary, other than a desire to receive the grace God pleases to give. No fitness or church membership is required at the time of communicating, other than recognizing our need for God's love, grace, and forgiveness. The Lord's Supper is ordinarily the meal of the baptized to renew one's baptismal covenant. In an extra-ordinary measure of God's hospitality, the Table is also open to all who seek God's healing and transformation. Therefore, if you want such grace as God pleases to give to you, draw near with faith, and as you prepare to receive this holy sacrament to your comfort and strength, make your sincere confession to almighty God.

Doxology

All stand; eucharistic elements and tithes are brought forward and placed on the Eucharist table.

Praise God from whom all blessings flow,
Praise him, all creatures here below;
Praise him above, ye heavenly host,
Praise Father, Son, and Holy Ghost

The Great Thanksgiving

Pastor: The Lord be with you.

People: And also with you.

Pastor: Lift up your hearts.

People: We lift them up to the Lord.

Minister: Let us give thanks to the Lord our God.

People: It is right to give our thanks and praise.

Pastor: It is right, and a good and joyful thing, always and everywhere to give thanks to you, Father almighty, Creator of heaven and earth. We thank you for sending your Son. We praise you for the sacrifice that he offered as an act of love to you and to the world on our behalf to take away the sins of the world. We thank you for opening your Table to us, those on the outside. We are part of your new creation. We are invited to the Table to live into this transformative resurrection grace. We praise you, God, Father, Son, and Holy Spirit. And so, with your people on earth and all the company of heaven, we praise your name and join their unending hymn.

All: Holy, holy, holy Lord, God of power and might, heaven and earth are full of your glory. Hosanna in the highest. Blessed is he who comes in the name of the Lord.

Pastor: Holy are you, and blessed is your Son, Jesus Christ. Your Spirit anointed him to preach good news to the poor, to proclaim release to the captives and recovery of sight to the blind, to set at liberty those who are oppressed, and to announce that the time had come when you would save your people. He healed the sick, fed the hungry, and ate with sinners. By the baptism of his suffering, death, and resurrection you gave birth to your church, delivered us from slavery to sin and death, and made with us a new covenant by water and the Spirit.

Institution Narrative

Pastor: On the night on which he gave himself up for us, our Lord Jesus took bread, gave thanks to you, broke the bread, gave it to his disciples, and said: "Take, eat; this is my body, which is given for you. Do this in remembrance of me." Likewise, when the supper was over, he took the cup, gave thanks to you, gave it to his disciples, and said: "Drink from this, all of you, this is my blood of the new covenant, poured out for you and for many for the forgiveness of sins. Do this, as often as you drink it, in remembrance of me." And so, in remembrance of these your mighty acts in Jesus Christ,

ALL: We offer ourselves in praise and thanksgiving as a holy and living sacrifice, in union with Christ's offering for us, as we proclaim the mystery of faith: Christ has died; Christ is risen; Christ will come again. He is risen! He is risen indeed!

Epiclesis

Pastor: Pour out your Holy Spirit on us gathered here, and on these gifts of bread and the cup. Make them be for us the body and blood of Christ, that we may be for the world the body of Christ, redeemed by his blood. By your Spirit make us one with Christ, one with each other, and one in ministry to all the world, until Christ comes in final victory and we feast at his heavenly banquet. Through your Son, Jesus Christ, with your Holy Spirit in your holy church, all honor and glory are yours, almighty Father, now and forever.

The Lord's Prayer

Pastor: And now, as our savior Christ has taught us, let us pray.

ALL: Our Father, who art in heaven, hallowed be thy name. Thy kingdom come, thy will be done on earth as it is in heaven. Give us this day our daily bread. And forgive us our trespasses as we forgive those who trespass against us. And lead us not into temptation, but deliver us from evil. For thine is the kingdom, and the power, and the glory, forever. Amen.

Appendix C: Communion Bread Recipe

This recipe for Communion bread seeks to exclude many ingredients that people are allergic or sensitive to. The only warning is that some do not like this bread because it tastes *too* good. The bread is both unleavened and gluten-free. This recipe is an adaptation of a Greek Orthodox recipe.

Preheat oven to 400 degrees Fahrenheit. Line a baking sheet with parchment paper.

2 cups all-purpose gluten-free flour
2 tsp baking powder
⅛ tsp salt
½ cup sugar
1½ tsp pumpkin pie spice
¼ cup milk
½ cup honey
2 tbsp vegetable oil

In separate bowls, mix together the dry ingredients and the wet ingredients. Add the mixture of wet ingredients to the dry mixture.

Roll the dough into 9 or 10 balls, place on the baking sheet, then flatten balls to about ¼ inch thick. If the mixture is too dry to roll, try adding up to 2 tbsp water, but don't overdo it.

Cover with parchment paper or flour. For larger loaves, roll out on pastry cloth or prepared surface. Using an 8–9" template (such as the lid of a pan) cut out a large loaf. Carefully transfer to baking sheet.

Using a spatula, carefully score a cross in the center of the loaf. Do not press all the way through the loaf. This not only places the symbol of the cross on top of the loaf but also allows for easier fracturing of the bread by the celebrant.

Bake in the oven 9 minutes. Loaf should be lightly browned. Cool completely before storing in a Ziploc bag.

Glossary of Theological Terms

The definitions of these terms are not comprehensive but specifically reflect how the Wesleyan sacramental tradition understands and uses them.

Baptism
A sacrament whereby God offers healing and salvation, both in forgiveness of sins (justification) and also in beginning the journey of healing in love (initial sanctification and new birth). This healing covenantally initiates us into the church, the body of Christ, and should be seen as the culmination (with the celebration of the Eucharist) of one's conversion into Christianity.

Catholic
The word by itself means universal. When capitalized, it has become shorthand for the Roman Catholic Church, but when it appears lowercased in prayers and creeds of the global church, it simply means universal.

Christian Perfection
See **Telos** and **Sanctification**

Confession
To admit we have done something wrong. In the Christian tradition, confession should always be connected to repentance.

Consecrate
To offer oneself to God to be set apart for God's purposes.

Doxology (Doxological)
Words of praise and thanksgiving to God.

Ecclesiology (Ecclesial)

Study and discourse about the church. The etymology from the Greek celebrates that *ekklesia* pertains to those who are *called out*. It is important not to see this as those called away from the world but as called to be set apart (holy) to better reflect God's image on the earth. As the church reflects God's image, we are called and sent by and with the Spirit to the world to participate in God's redemption of all things, including every tribe and nation.

Epiclesis

Literally, to "call upon, on, or around." Connects to the liturgical prayer in the sacrament of the Lord's Supper often called "The Great Thanksgiving." While the entire Eucharistic prayer requests the triune God to move and act, epiclesis asks the Father to make Christians and Christ uniquely present *by the Spirit*.

Eschatology (Eschatological)

Often called "end-times discourse," eschatology refers to the *already* of God's kingdom on earth and the *not yet* of the healing and redemption that is still to come. Christian eschatology is infused with hope and promise for what God has done, is doing, and will do.

Eucharist (Eucharistic)

Also called Communion or the Lord's Supper. One of two sacraments in the Wesleyan and greater Protestant tradition. Etymologically, it means "good grace." It also connotes the notion of thanksgiving. This term in the early church described the entire Christian communal worship service of Word and Table. In the last hundred years, it has often meant only the Table part of the communal service. At this meal, Christians are invited to become the body and blood of Christ by specifically encountering God's body and blood through the elements of bread and wine (or juice, as unfermented wine). In the Eucharist, we are invited to become what we partake—the body of Christ. As we offer ourselves, God transforms and heals us more fully to become the body of Christ.

Grace

The underserved, transforming, healing presence of God. This gift of God always *invites* and does not *coerce* our healing and transformation. It is important that we do not imagine grace as some object or substance we can hoard.

Holiness

See **Sanctification**

Image of God

Celebrates God's invitation to humanity to find joy in being loved by God, loving oneself, loving others, and taking responsibility for the flourishing of creation. Being created in the image of God is not a possession or a capacity given to humanity to own or control but an invitation offered by God into a journey of holy communion and deep joy.

Initial Sanctification

God's initial healing work on the journey of delivering people from the slavery and disease of sin. This term is sometime connected to the term "new birth."

Justification

Celebrates God's desire to forgive our sins and see us as righteous though the life, death, and resurrection of Jesus Christ. This is a juridical (legal) term referring to the way that persons were guilty of breaking the law because of sin. God removes that guilty status in light of the saving work of the triune God in Christ.

Kenosis (Kenotic)

Refers to self-emptying; often connects to the Christ hymn in Philippians 2. The triune God continually pours Godself out onto creation for the ongoing creating, sustaining, healing, and reconciling of all things.

Lord's Supper

See **Eucharist**

Martyr Ecclesiology

A celebration that the church is the body of the crucified and resurrected Christ. The martyr church does not seek to die but, in the hope of the resurrected Christ, is not afraid of it. It seeks to be a faithful witness (martyr) to Jesus Christ.

New Birth

Often associated with the healing God is working in the sacrament of baptism. It celebrates how persons are being born again, set free from the disease of sin into the healing of God's holy love.

Nominalism

Those who claim to be Christian but do not show the fruit or faith of the Christian gospel in their lives. In this sense, they are Christian in name only.

Oblation (Oblationary)

A sacrificial offering of thanksgiving to God. This offering is not about paying a debt or penalty but about offering oneself back to God in thanksgiving for all the healing God desires to give. In the Eucharist, we can only receive God's salvation as we offer ourselves back to God in thanksgiving. Jesus Christ offered his life back to the Father as an offering of thanksgiving. As Christ offers himself back to the Father, we too are invited to join this oblationary sacrifice most keenly at the Eucharist.

Ordo Salutis (Via Salutis)

Ordo means "order," and *via* means "way." *Salutis* refers to "salvation." *Ordo Salutis* celebrates that, while every journey is unique, there are similar steps on the Christian journey to move toward maturity in Christlikeness. Wesleyans celebrate God's first move in prevenient grace, which often leads to an awakening to sin and our need for God's forgiveness and healing. As we confess our sins and repent, God offers the gift of justification (legal declaration) and the new birth (the beginning of healing from sin to love). As we grow in grace, the Holy Spirit moves us toward entire consecration to God, whereby in God's timing we may experience a deeper infilling of the Holy Spirit in entire sanctification (also known as Christian perfection or perfect love). Sanctifying grace invites humans by the Spirit to keep maturing in love. After death, Christians can lean into full healing and restoration in glorification. A central conviction of this book is that all along the way, this ongoing healing and transformation are aided by practices of communal worship, prayer, and the sacraments. The key emphasis is to celebrate that God desires to heal and transform us from addiction and slavery to sin into reconciliation and healing in divine love.

Perichoresis (Perichoretic)

Means literally "to dance or move around." Refers to the divine dance of love within the Trinity. The Father, Son, and Spirit give and receive love in a place of joyful surrender.

Prevenient Grace

Celebrates God's work of healing that "comes before" to all persons. God's presence is continually wooing and drawing all persons unto Godself. God is always and continually making the first move, reaching out and inviting.

Repentance

Follows confession—our admission of sin. In repentance, we ask God to help change our behavior. The idea of repentance is also connected with having a change of mind and transformation.

Sacrament (Sacramental)

The Roman Catholic and Orthodox Christian traditions recognize seven sacraments: baptism, confirmation, Eucharist, penance (reconciliation), anointing the sick, marriage, and holy orders (ordination). The Protestant tradition recognizes two sacraments—baptism and the Eucharist. These are the actions commanded by Jesus as recorded in Scripture. To call something *sacramental* is to recognize that God can take things that are common and ordinary and use them to become occasions of healing and transformation. Hence, the world is infused with sacramental possibility.

Sacred-Secular Dualism

This unfortunate posture imagines some people and places to be holy, while other spaces, people, and objects are viewed as pagan or heathen (secular). This dualism works against the goodness of God's creation and the ability of God's universal presence to be always at work, seeking to redeem, restore, and renew.

Sanctification

Celebrates God's desire to *set persons apart* to better reflect God's image of love, joy, and hope to the world. God not only wants to forgive (justification) but also heal and transform people away from slavery to sin into a flourishing of love. Although sanctification is a work of the triune God, we must respond to the Spirit's empowerment to fully consecrate (set apart) all our lives to God.

Soteriology (Soteriological)

Pertains to the doctrine and conversation around Christian salvation.

Telos

Greek: "perfection, goal, aim, or purpose." Often translated as "perfection," which is a complicated word for modern Christians. Most

who imagine perfection think about being without flaw or blemish—
something that is static and can't change. This understanding is closer
to the Latin word *perfectum*. *Telos* is closer to the idea of something
that *fulfills* its goal, aim, or purpose. A video projector is perfect when
it is being used to project images. That projector could also be used
as a soccer ball. It might still work, but its use as a soccer ball would
likely damage its ability to be perfect (project images). Humans are
perfect (or, we achieve our *telos*) when we are being loved by God
and others and are loving God and others in return. This love and
perfection are dynamic. Perfection does not mean we will never make
another mistake.

Theosis

Can be defined as making persons divine, deification. For Wesleyans,
theosis celebrates humanity's renewal and remaking in the likeness of
God and being caught up into the triune dance of love.

Works of Mercy

Gracious and compassionate movements toward those entrusted
to our care. Some examples include acts of service like feeding the
hungry, providing shelter and clothing to the needy, being present
in times of pain or loneliness. It can also include sharing the gospel,
declaring God's forgiveness, joining in solidarity with cries of lament,
and celebrating God's transforming love and presence.

Works of Piety

Embodied practices connected to personal and communal worship.
Some examples include reading Scripture, praying, fasting, and participating in the sacraments.

Printed in the USA
CPSIA information can be obtained
at www.ICGtesting.com
LVHW010712191124
797000LV00003B/360